Industrial Restructuring in Mexico

Printed in the United States of America by
the Center for U.S.-Mexican Studies
University of California, San Diego

1993

Cover art:
Luis Guarnizo
"¿Un hombre nuevo? (A New Man?), 1991
Ink on paper
18 × 12 inches
(45.75 × 30.5 cm)
Courtesy of the artist

ISBN 1-878367-15-3

Contents

1 Introduction   1

2 The Monterrey Group and Its Relationship with
  the State   5
  The Emergence and Consolidation of an Industrial Empire
  Entrepreneurs and Government: Conflict and Reconciliation

3 Confronting the Crisis   15
  Emerging from the Crisis of 1982
  Financial Restructuring
  The Crisis of 1985–1986
  From Recovery to Growth

4 Gaining Entry to International Markets   29
  Producing for Export
  Obstacles to Trade with the United States
  Businessmen and NAFTA
  Partnerships and Coinvestments

5 Total Quality Programs and the New Labor
  Relations Model   63
  Quality Programs
  Labor Relations
  Trade Unionism in Monterrey Group Firms

6 Conclusion   83

Appendix 1   Composition of the Industrial Groups   91

Appendix 2   Plants Visited   99

Appendix 3   Management Boards, 1990   101

Appendix 4   CPNL Proposal for Reform of
             Constitutional Article 123   103

Acronyms List   105

References   107

About the Author   111

1

Introduction

The global economic crisis that began in the 1970s was initially viewed as an energy crisis and then as an international financial crisis; it is now increasingly recognized as a structural crisis of the production system. The industrial restructuring now under way to correct flaws in the system goes beyond transforming manufacturing firms to include the transformation of the entire system of relations of production and trade between countries. It is within this context that Mexico is redefining how its industry will enter the world economy.

Most studies of industrial restructuring in Mexico focus on large transnational industries, mainly in the automotive industry (see Carrillo 1990; Micheli 1991; Middlebrook 1991; Shaiken 1990, among others). This reflects, first, the importance of these firms within the Mexican economy; also, because of their links to parent firms abroad, transnationals are the first to react to changes in the national and international environments. Large domestic firms have received much less attention despite their prominence in the economic plans of the Salinas administration, which seeks to strengthen those national industries that demonstrate an ability to compete in international markets.

This volume seeks to fill this gap in the literature by taking up the issue of restructuring in large domestic industries; in it I examine a group of large firms in Monterrey, a major industrial city

My thanks to all who shared their time and knowledge in the interviews. My thanks also to the institutions that made this work possible: El Colegio de la Frontera Norte, the Universidad Autónoma de Nuevo León, the Fundación Friedrich Ebert, and the Center for U.S.-Mexican Studies at the University of California, San Diego, where I wrote this book while in residence as a Visiting Research Fellow. Lastly, I would like to thank my colleagues, without whose observations and careful readings of this manuscript the book would not have been possible.

in northeastern Mexico.[1] The strategies developed by these firms respond to the economic opening begun in Mexico in the 1980s. They are the threads in the new relationship being woven between Mexico and international markets; some of these new mechanisms for entering the world economy are exports, affiliation and joint investment with foreign firms, technology alliances, and supplier networks with clients in other countries.

The industries studied belong to the Monterrey Group (see table 1 and appendix 1), a 100-year-old industrial empire which almost succumbed to the economic crisis of the early 1980s.[2] The role that the Mexican state played in the amazing recovery of these industries and the state's new relationship with the country's entrepreneurial elites are key to understanding the actions these firms have pursued. The industries have taken advantage of state support to make a strong entry into international markets. My objective is to retrace the process by which these Monterrey industries were able to pull themselves out of the crisis and restructure their firms in the context of economic opening.

TABLE 1
CHARACTERISTICS OF THE MONTERREY GROUP CORPORATIONS

Group	Board President	General Director	Main Activity	Plants in Mexico	Assets*	# Workers
Alfa	Bernardo Garza Sada	Rafael Páez	Steel	27	3,080	28,000
Cemex	Marcelo Zambrano	Lorenzo Zambrano	Cement	22	3,050	13,840
Cydsa	Andrés Marcelo Sada	Fernando Sada Malacara	Chemical	18	800	9,163
Imsa	Eugenio Clariond Reyes	Eugenio Clariond Reyes	Galvanized Plate	SD	SD	10,000
Visa	Eugenio Garza Lagüera	Othón Ruiz Montemayor	Beer	39	1,800	40,000
Vitro	Adrián Sada	Ernesto Martens	Glass	37	4,332	46,000

* Millions of dollars. (Does not include firms acquired in 1992 and 1993)

Source: Bolsa Mexicana de Valores.

---

[1]Monterrey is 230 km. from Laredo, Texas, the closest U.S. border city, and 961 km. from Mexico City.

[2]The crisis in the pattern of accumulation based on import substitution began to take shape in the 1970s and was expressed at the start of the 1980s as a financial crisis: in 1981 and 1982, the public sector's net indebtedness rose to U.S. $33 billion; capital flight rose 884.6 percent in one year to reach at least $20 million. The value of the peso fell by 65 percent vis-à-vis the dollar in February 1982 and the peso was eventually devalued by 500 percent. The downward spiral led Mexico to declare a moratorium and initiate efforts to renegotiate its foreign debt (Garrido and Quintana 1988).

In chapter 2, I present a brief discussion of the origins and characteristics of Monterrey's industrial groups, as well as the evolution of their relationship with the state. The relationship, which was traditionally conflictive, has recently become one of close collaboration. Since the core of the research is the restructuring begun in the last decade, this historical section reviews studies carried out before relations began to change between this industrial group and the government.

In chapter 3 I reconstruct the activities of these companies during the 1980s, as well as the economic measures taken by the government during the same period. I then analyze the strategies that firms used to emerge from the crisis and to prepare to face the new conditions of the open economy, as well as the importance of governmental support in this process.

These companies' new export orientation has led them into a process of technological reconversion and reorganization of the production process, as well as a process of association and co-investment with foreign firms. These associations, as well as the problems of transfer, adaptation, and assimilation of new technology, are analyzed in the fourth chapter. Also examined are the attempts to introduce flexible management techniques; the new methods typically run up against old forms of command and the verticality of the previous systems.

Lastly, the analysis enters the heart of the labor issue: the new techniques of flexible organization of production require a new type of worker and contractual conditions that are much less rigid than the norm under Mexico's current labor legislation. In the fifth chapter, the effects of the reorganization of production on labor relations within the factories are analyzed in the context of the union structure prevailing in Mexico in general and in the Monterrey Group firms in particular, where so-called "white unions" predominate.

The analysis is based on observations and fieldwork that I and others carried out in three stages between 1990 and 1991.[3] During the first stage I interviewed sixteen division managers and department heads.[4] Those interviewed described the situation their firms experienced during the crisis and the strategies they followed to overcome it. This information was compared with data on the firms' financial situations, obtained through Infosel (a data bank of

---

[3] Partial results of the fieldwork appear in Pozas 1990, 1992a, 1992b, 1993.

[4] One group general manager; five division managers, one from each group; ten department heads, two from each group. I interviewed top firm management from Alfa, Cydsa, Vitro, Visa, and Imsa. The Cemex firm, which was involved in an antidumping suit, refused to be interviewed for security reasons.

the Monterrey newspaper *El Norte*), the Mexican stock exchange, business magazines, and national newspapers.[5]

In the second phase, taking the factory as the unit of analysis, we used a questionnaire on innovation and technology transfer to interview the heads of industrial engineering or research and development departments, where these existed. In some cases these questionnaires were combined with in-depth interviews with department heads. In the third stage, we visited plants and carried out in-depth interviews with a total of twelve supervisors and thirty workers drawn proportionally from those firms (see appendix 2).

While every researcher's analytical perspective is inevitably defined by the parameters of his or her discipline, it is increasingly necessary to draw on the explanatory strengths of other fields; this new practice carries the risk of oversimplification when handling multiple fields of knowledge. Nevertheless, in this work I opted to accept this risk and draw on literature generated by economists, sociologists of work, political scientists, and geographers. They share as their focus the reorganization of the production process currently unfolding worldwide, and their approaches range from the structural forms of the process studied by Piore and Sabel (1985), Boyer (1987, 1990), and Leborgne and Lipietz (1988) to the technological paradigms taken up by Dosi (1982), Mahon (1987), Schoenberger (1989a, 1989b) and the forms of organization of work studied by Gertler (1988), Locke (1990), and Simon (1990), among many others. However, it should be noted that this division is somewhat artificial, since all of them touch on all of these topics in one way or another.

---

[5]*Excélsior, Expansión,* CIEN (Centro de Información y Estudios Nacionales), *Calidad Total, Informe Anual del Banco de México, Análisis Económico, Información Financiera de Empresas Mexicanas* (SPP), *Examen de la Situación Económica de México* (BANAMEX), *La economía mexicana en cifras* (Nacional Financiera), among others.

2

The Monterrey Group and Its Relationship with the State

With neoliberalism ever more present in the political and economic discourse of industrialized country governments, the old polemic regarding the role of the state in the economy takes on renewed importance. In Europe the academic and political debate centers on the future of the welfare state; in Latin America the focus is the end of the period of protectionism and import substitution and the ascendance of economic opening which carries with it a reduction of state intervention in the economy.

In Mexico, the transformation of the state that accompanies economic opening and industrial restructuring has been understood by both government and private sector to mean reduced state intervention in the economy. The sale of a large number of parastatal firms and the reprivatization of the banks would seem to confirm the validity of this interpretation. However, this research points to significant state intervention in the new forms of accumulation that began to develop in Mexico after the 1982 crisis and to a new relationship between the state and the Mexican entrepreneurial elite, placing the interpretation in doubt.

A look at the Monterrey Group is an excellent means to approach this issue in an empirical manner, especially in light of the now close collaboration between the Monterrey entrepreneurs and the government. An analysis of the main economic policies implemented by the government in the 1980s and the actions undertaken by Monterrey Group firms during the same period reveals the hand of the state behind the restructuring process.

What is happening is that the Mexican state is no longer acting directly as an entrepreneur but is instead concentrating on designing and implementing a series of policies that deliberately orient economic activity toward exports and international markets. This state project implies altering the relationship that the state had maintained with the entrepreneurial sector for the last fifty years. Contradicting neoliberal postulates, the open economy toward which Mexico is headed entails close collaboration between the government and the entrepreneurial elite. Therefore, the elimination of subsidies and the lack of protection accorded to large industries are not what they appear. It is a matter instead of a new type of protection, which while including deregulation and economic opening, takes place in a framework of strict control over certain economic variables that could harm the firms. It is for this reason that the implementation of neoliberal-inspired policies takes place together with control over prices and wages and over interest and exchange rates.

The case of the Monterrey Group illustrates the two fundamental premises that underlie this changing relationship between the Mexican state and big capital: First, what is in crisis is not state intervention in the economy, but the *specific form of intervention* that prevailed until the early 1980s. Second, the type of relationship between government and the business sector is modified so that a new alliance replaces the secular conflict between the two sectors. But before analyzing this conflict-ridden relationship in detail, it is pertinent to lay out some historical facts on the origin and evolution of the Monterrey Group.

THE EMERGENCE AND CONSOLIDATION OF AN INDUSTRIAL EMPIRE

Monterrey's entrepreneurs make up one of the oldest industrial groups in Mexico. Their appearance in the nineteenth century allowed them to consolidate and unify as a class much earlier than other Mexican entrepreneurs. The fortunes concentrated in Monterrey between 1850 and 1890 were invested in industry and mining; during the Porfiriato these entrepreneurs benefited from their links in the domestic market and their geographic proximity to the U.S. market. They were also favored by the development of the railroads, which made Monterrey one of the cities best connected to the rest of Mexico and to the United States. Lastly, the policies implemented under Nuevo León governor Bernardo Reyes[6] favored all kinds of investment, especially factory investment, and attracted foreign capital, especially U.S. capital. These and other conditions made this capital city of Nuevo León an important center of regional development and made its entrepre-

---

[6]Bernardo Reyes governed Nuevo León almost without interruption from 1885 to 1909.

neurs one of the strongest economic groups in the country (Cerutti 1983).

Two large industries that developed at the end of the nine-teenth century gave rise to what is today known as the Monterrey Group. The first is the Cervecería Cuauhtémoc, a brewery founded in 1881 with capital from the Calderón y Cía. merchant house and from Isaac Garza, Francisco Sada, and José Muguerza. In 1899 the brewery began to expand vertically by establishing glass, paper, cardboard, and bottle cap factories. Later it diversified its interests, expanding into the steel sector (Hojalata y Lámina in 1942) and the chemical sector (Celulosa y Derivados in 1945). It also went into banking and financial services and gave rise to what was then called the Cuauhtémoc Group, led by Eugenio Garza Sada until his death in 1973. In 1974, the group was divided into four large holding companies controlled by descendants of the founding families: Alfa (Bernardo Garza Sada), Visa (Eugenio Garza Lagüera), Vitro (Adrián Sada), and Cydsa (Andrés Marcelo Sada). All were among the twelve largest industrial groups in the country, and despite having expanded into other states of Mexico, still retain their base of operations in Monterrey (see appendix 1). The other pioneer firm in the process of industrial development in the region was the Fundidora de Fierro y Acero de Monterrey, founded in 1910. However, this firm later became state property and was declared bankrupt in 1986.

Over the course of a century other important industries ap-peared: the Santos Group held interests in the food industry and in 1990 sold 80 percent of its most important firm to Pepsico; the Ramírez Group, involved in the tractor-trailer sector of the motor vehicle industry; the Cemex Group, probably the largest cement exporter in Mexico; and the Imsa Group, producer of galvanized plate. Cemex and Imsa are headed by Lorenzo Zambrano and Eugenio Clariond Reyes, respectively.

The Monterrey industrial empire gave rise to an elite made up of interlocking financial and commercial interests and leadership personnel exchanges. Further, the establishment of family ties between the descendants of the founders meant that for many years Monterrey business was essentially a "family matter" (Sar-agoza 1988; Cerutti 1983).

Monterrey industry developed with links to both domestic and foreign markets, giving precedence to one or another orientation depending on the varying economic conjunctures throughout the twentieth century. After World War II and as a result of the protectionism and the policy of import substitution in Mexico, the Monterrey firms organized their production primarily around the domestic market.

This study focuses on six corporations in the Monterrey Group: Alfa, involved in steel, petrochemical, paper, packaging, and food production; Cemex, a cement firm that holds 69 percent of the Mexican market; Cydsa, specializing in chemicals, cellophane film, and acrylic fibers; Imsa, a producer of galvanized plate, batteries, and steel products; Visa, involved in the beverage (beer and soft drinks) and food industries; and Vitro, a corporation specializing in glass production but which also has rubber, plastics, machinery, and chemical plants. Together, these corporations own more than 143 manufacturing plants throughout the country,[7] and their assets total more than U.S. $13 billion (see table 1 and appendix 1).

These firms' prosperity nearly ended in 1982, when their heavy indebtedness and Mexico's high inflation rates brought them to the brink of bankruptcy. However, as we shall see in the next chapter, the firms undertook a series of strategies which, along with strong support from the federal government, enabled them to survive the crisis and grow once again. The government's help surprised the public because Monterrey businessmen's relations with the state had been conflictual practically since the turn of this century. The historic evolution of this relationship, which has been documented by Cerutti (1983), Vellinga (1981), Nuncio (1982), and others, takes on a different meaning in light of the events of the last decade and the rapid process of Mexico's opening.

ENTREPRENEURS AND GOVERNMENT:
CONFLICT AND RECONCILIATION

The bulk of the present-day entrepreneurial class in Mexico arose under the wing of the postrevolutionary government, which from the outset offered entrepreneurs protection and encouraged their dependence on the state. However, the Monterrey enterprises did not follow this pattern. Because their origin dates from the nineteenth century, they evolved separately from the regime that arose from the 1910 Revolution. This explains why their outlook differs so radically from that of businessmen in central Mexico (Cerutti 1983). The Monterrey Group voiced strong opposition to government policies that went against their interests and put a regionalist stamp on its actions. This has been visible historically in the continuous tension between industrialists trying to achieve regional autonomy and the central government trying to affirm its higher authority. On several occasions this tension has blossomed into conflict, as in 1916 when the Cuauhtémoc Brewery was taken over by revolutionaries in reprisal for the political stance of its

---

[7]This figure does not include their commercial and service firms.

owners. The owners left Mexico and remained abroad until the firm was returned to them in 1919.

During this period the bases were laid for what would be a peculiar relationship between the government and the Mexican entrepreneurial class. While government protects the interests of the capitalist class generally, at the same time it remains subordinated—at least formally—to the consensus of the popular sectors. Although the Mexican Constitution of 1917 incorporated the demands of the workers and peasants who fought in the Mexican Revolution, the national project that took shape in the Constitution was a capitalist project. The postrevolutionary state simultaneously laid the foundations for the development of industry and cemented its links to the groups that brought it to power. The result was a strong and highly centralized state which attempted to resolve the contradiction between its nationalist interests and the interests of individual capitalists through policies that placed businessmen and their goods at the service of so-called national goals. Unfortunately these national goals did not always coincide with those of the large industrialists.

The ways that Mexican businessmen responded to this situation gave rise to two business factions. The Monterrey Group falls into the oldest, "radical" faction, based primarily in the north and maintaining an apparent autonomy vis-à-vis the central government. The other large faction was the "moderates," located primarily in the metropolitan areas of the Valley of Mexico. They developed their firms under the open protection and with the direct support of the postrevolutionary government; they have, therefore, been much less independent historically (Tirado 1987).

Despite this division within the business elite, government protectionism and the policy of import substitution benefited the whole of national industry equally. Aside from some especially conflict-ridden moments, Monterrey businessmen participated in the tacit agreement established between the Mexican government and domestic business after 1940. This agreement was based on a clear separation of functions: politics and government would be the prerogative of the political class, and business would produce. Even so, on repeated occasions the Monterrey Group turned belligerent when an administration's policies were perceived as contrary to their interests. This occurred during the administrations of Lázaro Cárdenas (1934–40), Adolfo López Mateos (1958–64), and Luis Echeverría (1970–76), all of whom carried out policies favorable to workers and popular sectors and were branded as "populists" by business.

In general terms, the relationship between the central government and the Monterrey business elite has gone through three clearly identifiable stages: the period of intermittent pressure, which goes from 1929 until 1969; the stage of radical political opposition, which developed during the 1970s; and a growing convergence in the 1980s, culminating in the present alliance between this business group and the Salinas administration.

The first stage began with a heated conflict in 1929 over the shape of the labor law that would flesh out Article 123 of the Constitution. That year, COPARMEX (the Business Federation of Mexico) was founded at the initiative of the Monterrey Group in order to protect the private sector from the state's drive to control relations between capital and labor and thus to intervene in business (Rojas 1983). The law was finally promulgated in 1931, and business hastened to promote the growth of company ("white") unions in order to deflect any interference by the state or leftist groups (see chapter 5).

The administration of President Lázaro Cárdenas in the 1930s marks the period of greatest distance between the federal government and the Monterrey businessmen, who opposed Cárdenas's reformist policies. In 1936, the conflict between Cárdenas and the Monterrey business sector became public when the president intervened in favor of the workers during a strike at Vidriera (a firm belonging to the Cuauhtémoc Group). Cárdenas issued harsh warnings to the businessmen who rejected his project to develop the industrial sector, as well as his proposal for a corporative form of labor organization (Nuncio 1982).

During the 1940s Monterrey business attempted to gain control of state and city government, resulting in a series of conflicts. Among the most notable were the attacks against Governor Arturo B. de la Garza (1943–49),[8] especially after the works of the Monterrey Water and Sewerage Company (formerly in the hands of a Canadian firm) were handed over to the government (Nuncio 1984; Bennett 1987). Relations became even tenser after the federal government put Cristalería, another of the Cuauhtémoc Group firms, in receivership.

The 1950s were marked in Mexico by important trade union mobilizations—foremost among them those of teachers and railroad workers. The government's repression of these movements let business stay aloof from the conflicts. In contrast, during the 1960s, under the López Mateos government, problems between the federal government and Monterrey businessmen resurfaced when the government nationalized the electrical power industry and refused to follow the United States' lead in a trade blockade against Cuba.

---

[8]Not related to the Garza Sada family. The Garza surname is very common in the region.

It was during this same period that the government introduced a single national textbook and a 1 percent tax for education (Nuncio 1984).

Under Echeverría the differences between Monterrey businessmen and the central government reached their apex. Echeverría's attempts to carry out deep reforms, precisely when Mexico's economy was destabilizing somewhat after a prolonged period of sustained growth, were intolerable to businessmen, who heard clear leftist tendencies in Echeverría's words. When added to the social and political instability of that period, Echeverría's policies provoked a violent reaction from the business sector. At the time, Monterrey was undergoing a veritable social crisis in which several movements coincided: the university community's struggle for autonomy, which led in 1972 to the resignation of Governor Eduardo Elizondo, a close ally of the business sector (Ibarra 1984); the appearance of the "Land and Liberty" squatters' commune, whose anticapitalist stance was perceived as a direct attack on the principle of private property (Garza and Pérez 1984; Pozas 1990); the mobilizations of important trade unions such as the mine and metal workers, the telephone workers, and the electrical workers, among others; and the urban guerrilla actions that took the form of bank robberies, an airplane hijacking, and the attempted kidnapping of Eugenio Garza Sada, head of the Cuauhtémoc Group and Monterrey business leader, which ended with his death in 1973.[9] These events provoked a spirited reaction from the Monterrey bourgeoisie, who spoke out against what they considered to be "social chaos and a total lack of authority" (Nuncio 1984). At the same time, the businessmen's reaction encased deep opposition to an economic policy which they viewed as an attack on their interests. Thus, they opposed Echeverría's project for a thoroughgoing fiscal reform and emergency wage increases, as well as price controls and plant inspections (Nuncio 1984).

Even less acceptable to the businessmen was that by decreeing his reforms, Echeverría had violated the tacit agreement between government and business, i.e., that any decision that affected business should be preceded by private consultations and negotiations at the highest level of the business elite. In response, businessmen threatened to stop paying federal taxes and to freeze their investments. Their impressive economic power was once again their principal political weapon. The actions of the Monterrey businessmen produced a united business class at a national level, with enough strength to reverse or modify the government's

---

[9]For a detailed analysis of the conflicts between the state and Monterrey businessmen, see Nuncio 1984.

reformist initiatives. The historic division of functions between politicians and businessmen gave way to the businessmen's political will to assume a leading role in national decision making across the board (Tirado 1987).

The tranquility which seemed to return with the oil boom and the arrival of José López Portillo to the presidency in 1976 shattered in 1982 with the onset of a crisis that had been brewing over the previous decade. It led López Portillo to declare the country nearly bankrupt, with its reserves exhausted and unable to pay its external debt. This forced Jesús Silva Herzog, minister of the treasury, to seek help in Washington. He found it, in exchange for accepting certain measures proposed by the IMF. In his last State of the Nation address in September 1982, López Portillo nationalized Mexican banks in an attempt to regain control over the country's chaotic financial situation. However, most of the affected Monterrey business and financial groups did not react with the anticipated vengeance despite the direct harm the bank nationalization dealt to their property. They patiently awaited the response of president-elect Miguel de la Madrid, who provided a satisfactory resolution to the conflict: a new private financial system in stock brokerage houses and the reprivatization of 34 percent of the stock in Mexican banks. He also gave businessmen legal guarantees that there would be no future nationalizations without the approval of Congress.

Although businessmen from the radical faction (primarily from Chihuahua) did oppose the bank nationalization, their movement had already lost its most powerful representatives. When the government confirmed that bank services would remain exclusively in the hands of the state, a part of the now divided radical faction rejected the bases upon which the government was seeking to renew its alliance with the business sector. This group, supported by the Catholic church and the opposition National Action Party (PAN), spread their version of the crisis, which relieved the business sector of any responsibility and blamed the crisis entirely on a corrupt and inept government and political bureaucracy (Tirado 1987).

The changing stance of the Monterrey business elite, which had gone from the belligerence of the 1970s to the acceptance of the bank expropriation, was largely due to the fact that the crisis had brought its firms to the brink of bankruptcy, as we shall see in the next chapter. The fact that the government was giving them strong support in order to avoid this eventuality[10] significantly modified

---

[10]Alfa, for example, in 1981 had to request a loan from President José López Portillo in order to avoid bankruptcy (see chapter 3).

the attitude of the most important businessmen in the group toward the government.

Only a few Monterrey industrialists, those least impacted by the crisis, decided to turn (for the first time) to electoral means to express their discontent. In 1985 the PAN nominated Fernando Canales Clariond, a member of the Imsa board, for governor of Nuevo León. The PAN's popularity reached its peak in the state that year. However, with most leaders of the radical faction no longer active, the PAN declined in Monterrey after the election. In fact, in the presidential elections of 1988 Monterrey was one of the few urban areas in Mexico where the PRI victory was beyond question.

In this state, generally considered to be a bastion of the PAN, this result can only be explained by the increasing convergence between the economic policy of the de la Madrid government and the businessmen's project, as well as by the rapprochement cultivated with Monterrey business by then-presidential-candidate Carlos Salinas de Gortari, who held a series of closed-door meetings with the city's business elite. On the other hand, the electoral behavior of the general population spoke to the tremendous influence of the business sector and its capacity to assume the role of political leadership in the state.

To summarize, there are three stages in the relationship between the state and the Monterrey Group throughout this century. The first, covering up to the end of the 1960s, is a period during which the business sector expressed its political actions primarily as a pressure group. Thus, this business faction reaffirmed its presence at times of conflict but practically disappeared during periods of social peace (Tirado 1987). In the second stage—the 1970s—when business perceived a significant risk in the reformist discourse of President Luis Echeverría, the Monterrey Group reacted violently against government policy and assumed a leadership role at the national level with the formation of the Business Coordinating Council (the CCE). The third stage, which began after 1982, is characterized by the convergence in discourse and economic policy between business and the state and by their increasing collaboration, as shall be seen later.

The features of the state-Monterrey Group relationship were transformed on the basis of changes in the government project: from a populist policy originating in the revolutionary period and based on capitalist accumulation via import substitution and protection of national industry, to the state's current economic opening and export orientation. The new model makes both actors recognize that they need one another as they come face to face with foreign capital and international competition; this does not necessarily mean reduced state intervention in economic affairs. A closer look at this convergence is the subject of the following chapter.

3

Confronting the Crisis

The Mexican government's effort to shape a new development model has been long and arduous; it has come in response to the crisis in the import substitution model and the country's enormous external debt, which in 1982 seemed to deny any possibility for economic growth over the short or medium term. Among the many expressions of the crisis, the country went through a process of deindustrialization; as a result manufacturing production dropped by 2.4 percent from 1981 to 1982, and by more than 7 percent from 1982 to 1983 (Story 1990: 50). Nevertheless, between 1981 and 1986 a small number of manufacturing firms—those linked to the export sector—were able to increase the volume and value of their production. Their success influenced the administration's economic policy, orienting it toward promoting the highly productive export sector, with the hope that the benefits would trickle down to the population as a whole.

This process has acted as a screening mechanism which eliminates all but the most modern and dynamic sectors, those with the ability to compete in the world market. Recent data from the National Chamber of Manufacturers (CANACINTRA) indicate that by the end of 1991 one-fourth of Mexico's productive plant had been left behind: sixteen of a total of forty-eight manufacturing subsectors have not even been able to reattain the production volumes they had in 1981. These sixteen subsectors generate 25 percent of factory employment (900,000 jobs) and include over one-fourth of manufacturing-sector firms.

Therefore the gap between large industry (which makes up barely 2.6 percent of the country's industrial establishments) and small and medium industry tends to grow wider.[11] The recovery and successful restructuring of the large Monterrey firms, decisively backed by the governing team since 1982, provides an extraordinary illustration of this process.

As noted earlier, Alfa, Vitro, Cydsa, Visa, Imsa, and Cemex are outstanding among the large Monterrey companies because, despite having been hard hit by the crisis in 1982, they had achieved an extraordinary recovery by the end of the decade. These companies combined favorable state policy with deep-going changes in their production and organizational strategies, taking advantage of the external opening promoted by Presidents Miguel de la Madrid and Carlos Salinas de Gortari.

Like most large firms in Mexico, the Monterrey business groups had taken advantage of the 1980–81 oil boom to achieve spectacular growth rates: the assets of these groups increased 22 percent in only one year, to U.S. $10.46 billion in 1981.[12] Alfa and Visa represented 63 percent of that total. During Mexico's boom years, profits and bank financing were insufficient to finance the groups' expansion projects, and this led them to turn increasingly to international (especially North American) banks, rapidly running up their external debt. Between 1978 and 1981, Visa increased its debt in national currency by 64 percent and its debt in foreign currency by 562 percent. For Vitro the figures were 90 and 865 percent, respectively. Alfa's external debt grew by 468 percent (CIEN 1983).

When the crisis erupted, the debt of the Monterrey groups as a whole was close to $6 billion: Alfa's debt reached $2.7 billion; Visa's, $2.3 billion; Vitro's, $600 million; and Cydsa's, nearly $400 million (*Expansión* 1983).

Company adjustments included massive worker layoffs, which contributed to a 9.8 percent unemployment rate in Monterrey in 1983, the highest in Mexico (BANAMEX 1987). Alfa had to cut back its personnel by 34 percent, laying off more than 17,000 workers between 1981 and 1983 out of a total of about fifty thousand (see table 2). Furthermore, it sold off a large number of firms which it had founded or bought (primarily producers of capital goods and home appliances), reducing its assets by almost 40 percent in those years (*Expansión* 1983). Vitro reduced its work force by almost 36 percent from 1980 levels of more than thirty thousand workers by laying off close to eleven thousand employees. Its capacity utilization dropped from 90 percent in the boom years to less than

---

[11] The INEGI classification counts firms with more than one hundred employees as large industry.

[12] Amounts are in current dollars.

70 percent in 1983. In mid-1983, Cydsa was operating at 60 percent capacity after suspending operations at several of its plants due to a scarcity of imported raw materials (CIEN 1983).

TABLE 2
EVOLUTION OF THE EMPLOYMENT IN MONTERREY GROUP FIRMS

Group	1977	1980	1982	1989	1991
Alfa	19,505	49,019	33,951	28,600	28,000
Visa	24,068	48,032	34,403	40,266	40,000
Vitro	24,096	36,616	27,373	45,770	46,000
Cydsa	4,766	8,213	8,249	9,048	9,163
Cemex	NA	4,082	5,298	14,000	13,840

Source: Centro de Información y Estudios Nacionales. The 1977–1982 data come from each firm's yearly reports.

Groups such as Cemex and Imsa, which had grown conservatively during the boom years and were not heavily indebted, were in a better position to face the crisis. Nevertheless, they too were deeply affected, essentially because of the drastic contraction of the domestic market.

EMERGING FROM THE CRISIS OF 1982

Between 1982 and 1985, the economic policy outlined in the Economic Recovery Program (PIRE) institutionalized the government's intention to promote growth based not solely on the domestic market but also on an efficient economy able to compete in the international market. Financial institutions changed ownership, and a series of institutional reforms transformed the financial circuits of surplus capital and control over it until the collapse of the program in 1985 (Garrido and Quintana 1988).

During this period, most of the groups postponed or canceled their growth projects and limited their investments to what was essential to keep their installations operating (parts, inputs, and working capital). Their main concern was to renegotiate their external debt and reduce their liabilities, as well as to increase productivity. This resulted in even larger worker layoffs (CIEN 1983).

On the government policy side, the PIRE helped by producing a sharp drop in real wages. This allowed a significant increase in available surplus so that payment commitments on the external debt could be met. In only one year (1983), wages lost 24.6 percent of their buying power compared to the previous year (see figure 1) (CNSM 1989).

Figure 1
Real Wage Levels in the Industrial Sector
1980-1989

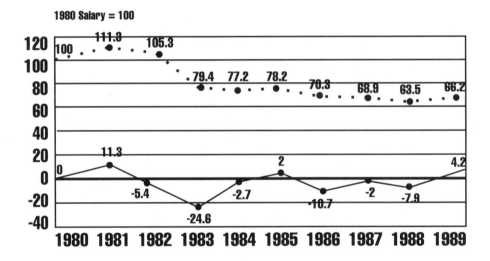

1980 Salary = 100

···· Salary level   ⸺ Percent variation

Sources: Nora Lustig, "PRONASOL as a Strategy of Poverty Alleviation," presentation at the research workshop, "Mexico's National Solidarity Program (PRONASOL): A Preliminary Assessment," Center for U.S.-Mexican Studies, UCSD, La Jolla, CA, February 25, 1992; CNSM; INEGI.

For Monterrey industry the 1982 crisis was not only a financial crisis but also a crisis in strategy: the development blueprint that the firms had followed in the previous decade was abandoned in order to concentrate anew on the products they had manufactured originally. During the 1970s, these groups had based their development on high rates of growth, expansion, and diversification into highly dynamic and profitable subsectors and products,[13] and on increasingly complex forms of organization and integration—all underpinned by high levels of external debt.

The case of Alfa is significant: between 1976 and 1982, this corporation ventured into practically every sector of the economy, and by the end of the 1970s it had achieved growth rates of up to 30 percent (CIEN 1983). At the same time, the image of success that it was able to project through extremely splashy expenditures gave it access to the large sums it needed to modernize its plants and to buy a large number of firms, not all of which proved to be in good financial condition. Early warning signals appeared in 1980 with a drop in stock values and a 5 percent decrease in profits. By mid-1981 Alfa showed losses of $255 million. By October 1981, this most fervent opponent of state intervention in the economy was forced to ask President López Portillo for a loan of $480 million, which was extended through the National Public Works Bank (BANOBRAS). Despite such a substantial infusion of capital, Alfa's losses approached $6 billion in 1982. In April 1982 Alfa suspended payments on the principal on its $2.3 billion in debt and was then forced to turn over 45 percent of its stock to creditors from foreign banks. From that moment on, Alfa began to drown in debt. Its situation was exacerbated by the onset of the 1982 crisis, which led to a drastic contraction of Mexico's domestic market and the rapid deterioration of its terms of trade. That year Alfa unveiled a new strategy for debt repayment, which consisted of creating a *new* Alfa based on its most profitable firms, including Hylsa and the petrochemical companies Petrocel, Nylon, Fiqsa, and Polioles. As was noted by an Alfa vice president: "Our diversification plans of the 1970s and early 1980s had to be thrown out, burned" (*Business Week*, November 1989).

As for Visa, during the boom it sought to diversify its risk by expanding from beer and packaging into soft drinks, tourism, food, construction, etc. These ventures turned out not to be profitable; Visa's lack of experience in the new subsectors and the fact that resources had to be spread thin prevented Visa from

---

[13] Alfa and Visa diversified into a wide range of activities, while Vitro and Cydsa expanded into categories and product lines closely related to their areas of operation.

getting the same returns it realized in its traditional lines. By the end of 1982, Visa reported losses of $111 million.

While Alfa and Visa carried out their expansions by acquiring existing firms or groups, Vitro and Cydsa opted to start new firms and expand or modernize ones they already owned. Vitro even got a head start in the globalization that would prevail at the end of the decade when it entered into association with firms such as Ford and Anchor Glass Container. This strategy allowed Vitro to obtain the foreign exchange it needed to meet its liabilities in dollars, and even made possible the purchase of Troqueles y Esmaltes in 1984. This latter firm, which was practically bankrupt, became Vitro's Domestic Appliances Division. However, the main effect of the crisis for Vitro was a dramatically contracted domestic market for glass. It therefore sought to diversify its markets, making forays into Europe and Central and South America. In contrast, Cemex's expansion over the last two decades was not so closely linked to diversification, but aimed rather at gaining control over the Mexican cement market. In the space of twenty years (1966–87) Cemex was able to eliminate the competition by buying up practically all competing firms.

Despite the groups' different situation, one strategy common to all was to sell shares in firms that were no longer profitable. Another was management reorganization: the high degree of centralization in decision making was modified so that subsidiaries gained greater autonomy in their management. Some administrative departments were reduced in size or even eliminated; others grew, reflecting the new corporate orientation. For example, while once-small export departments began to grow, centralized planning departments became less important. Under the new conditions, departments that sought out firms to purchase in the boom period were reoriented toward renegotiating the debt.

Another key element of the reorganization process was the professionalization of corporate boards, which traditionally had been in the hands of the founding families. In the case of Alfa, for example, Bernardo Garza Sada was replaced as the head of the corporation by Rafael R. Páez; at Visa, Eugenio Garza Lagüera gave his place to Othón Ruiz Montemayor; at Vitro, Ernesto Martens replaced Adrián Sada. The new general managers were distinguished by their education in universities abroad. The old leaders kept their positions as chairmen of the board and have so far retained control of their companies. This despite the fact that the makeup of the boards has also changed as they were opened to include businessmen who were not family members. This is true especially in Vitro, Alfa, Cydsa, and Visa (see appendix 3). This recomposition is very important because it gave rise to one of the major outcomes of the 1980s crisis: the modification of the hege-monic groups and the configuration of new business blocs in Mexico. Businessmen from other regions of the country (primarily from Mexico City and México State) now make up part of the boards of the Monterrey industrial firms. In turn, the Monterrey businessmen are also on the boards of companies in other parts of Mexico. Frequently these recompositions are the result of mergers of large firms, as in the merger of the Cuauhtémoc and Moctezuma breweries in 1987, making both of them Visa firms.

The process to transform the hegemonic groups quickened toward the end of the decade when the reprivatization of the banks and the sale of state-owned firms stimulated the formation of new alliances and associations, above all because of the size of the firms up for sale and the resources required to buy them. In various regions, capital came together in order to participate in the eco-nomic spaces that the state was ceding to the private sector. Even those Monterrey groups least affected by the crisis—due to their conservative strategy during the 1970s, and which until recently had kept traditional organizational schemes—are also instituting changes as a result of the reprivatization process. An example is Imsa, a steel corporation whose management board is still strictly made up of members of the family circle (see appendix 3). But in order to buy the parastatal firm Aceros Planos, Imsa allied itself with the Duferco group and Villacero, which had acquired the parastatal firms of Altos Hornos de México, S.A. (AHMSA) and Sicartsa (Siderúrgica Lázaro Cárdenas-Las Truchas, S.A.). This acquisition led Imsa to create a new firm (Ampsa) with its own board of directors, although Imsa has kept control (*El Porvenir*, November 23, 1991; *El Norte*, November 23 and 26, 1991).

The spread of the Monterrey Group's plants and divisions to almost all of Mexico has been another means to include new stockholders. Exchanges resulting from stockholders' meetings have encouraged the formation of a communications and decision-making network which helps transmit experiences and homoge-nize strategies among the country's largest firms; at the same time these exchanges have favored the concentration of capital in the hands of a more united elite with increased power to influence the direction of Mexico's economic policy.

FINANCIAL RESTRUCTURING

Another key aspect of government support for the recovery of the industrial groups took place in the realm of finances. In 1983, the federal government created the Exchange Rate Risk Trust Fund (FICORCA) as a financial mechanism to rescue indebted firms.

The firms' debts, protected by FICORCA, were restructured, converted to pesos, and paid to the Banco de México according to a controlled exchange rate that differed significantly from the market exchange rate. This assured that the slide in the exchange rate on the free market would not affect the cost of the external debt. Furthermore, this system allowed payments to be made by stages, counteracting increases due to inflation; it even made it possible to save in the payment of taxes on the total cost of the debt. The nationwide, privately held debt assumed by FICORCA came to $12 billion (*Expansión* 1987). Eighty percent of FICORCA's total resources were concentrated in no more than twenty national groups and large firms (Garrido and Quintana 1988). Among them were all the corporations we have been discussing. For example, FICORCA assumed 55 percent of the external debt of Hylsa— Alfa's most important and most indebted firm (*El Norte*, May 5, 1990).

The importance that nonpetroleum export promotion policies began to have was reflected in 1983 in the creation of the National Program to Promote Foreign Trade (PRONAFICE). The Monterrey firms that had already begun to turn toward export markets were among the best prepared to take advantage of the government's stimulus packages and export subsidies and to adapt to what was becoming the new axis of accumulation: foreign demand.

Visa, for example, had diversified its exports and in 1982 sold beer for the first time to Holland, Japan, and Africa. That same year, Vitro exported $27.7 million worth of flat glass and increased its foreign sales of glass containers. Cydsa began to increase exports beginning in 1981; by the end of 1982 they had risen by 125 percent (*Expansión* 1983). At Imsa, exports grew from practically zero in 1981 to nearly 40 percent of production in 1985.

The marked contraction of the domestic market and the subsequent currency devaluations produced by the new economic policy, designed to make Mexican products more competitive in international markets, were additional factors contributing to this significant increase in exports. Another element that the businessmen themselves view as key to the speed with which Monterrey industries turned their production abroad is the fact that exporting was not something new to them. At various times in the past, before the import substitution period, they had maintained close trade relations with the United States. As one prominent businessman noted, "we simply organized to export again." In his view, most industries located in the Mexico City metropolitan area did not have this previous experience; because their mind-set was oriented solely toward the domestic market, they had greater difficulties. Indeed, Monterrey businessmen had to work hard to convince their subsidiaries in México State that exporting had become a necessity.

THE CRISIS OF 1985–1986

In 1985 there was a drastic reduction in total exports: during the first six months of that year, exports declined by 10 percent from the same period the year before, falling from $10.4 billion to $9.4 billion (*Expansión* 1986). This decline was largely due to the confluence of various factors. A decline in international demand for and the price of oil and primary products was one. Others were a stronger dollar and increasing U.S. protectionism, which strangled the ability of Mexican products to compete. In 1986 manufacturing GDP declined once again, this time by 5.6 percent (De la Garza 1988), while wages suffered a drastic fall (see figure 1).

Government policy was oriented toward restructuring the financial system, establishing the bases to configure a new system around the stock brokerage houses and to allow the reinsertion of the owners of capital into the banking circuit. However, the participation of various actors in the struggle over control of the surplus— among them the transnational banks and the technocrats recently arrived in the government sector—provoked a series of extraordinary tensions, aggravated by the capital flight which benefited transnational banks. This created the conditions for the appearance of the 1985 debt crisis (Garrido et al. 1987).

The response was a change in economic policy. The PIRE was transformed into the Stimulus and Growth Program (PAC), which was based on the recognition (expressed by President de la Madrid) of "the impossibility of continuing a policy of paying the debt while sacrificing economic growth." In July 1985, de la Madrid announced the implementation of "dynamic and thorough economic policy measures to face the challenges and adverse circumstances that have made the country's old problems more acute" (*Comercio Exterior* 1985).

Faced with this second phase of the crisis, the only alternative seemed to be to intensify changes in the economic structure within the framework of the neoliberal agenda: in a very short time Mexico agreed to enter GATT, reduced tariff and nontariff trade barriers to imports, and implemented an important tax reform. These measures resulted in a period of surplus budgets which enabled the government to renegotiate the debt despite the fact that it had not structurally solved the problem, since the surpluses were based on deeply depressed wages and a radical reduction of public spending.

Nevertheless, these apparently optimistic conditions sparked an unprecedented rise in the Mexican stock market in 1987, followed by a crash in October of that same year. In the midst of the threat of hyperinflation, capital flight, and wage indexing, the government was forced to regain equilibrium by means of wage and price controls through the Economic Solidarity Pact (PSE). The PSE was a concertation mechanism which included representatives of government, the private sector, and labor. This new crisis exposed the weakness of a project based essentially on financial strategies and on the precarious equilibrium of the expectations of capitalists who, seeing no real investment options, constantly threatened to take their capital out of the country.

However, the practice of the Monterrey businessmen differed somewhat from this pattern. For them 1987 was a turning point, after which they moved from recovery strategies to investment and development projects. The factor that made this transition possible was that the firms were able, with the support of the state's economic and financial policy, to rid themselves of most of their external debt.

FROM RECOVERY TO GROWTH

The convergence of a series of factors allowed the Monterrey groups to complete the restructuring of their debt in 1988 and free up the resources they needed for renewed growth. Most important was freezing the dollar, which held constant the amount of interest the firms paid to service the external debt (since FICORCA allowed them to make payments in national currency). Because inflation was around 50 percent while the dollar was devalued by less than 3 percent measured in pesos, these payments declined sharply in real terms (*El Norte*, March 3, 1989).

A second factor that benefited the Monterrey firms was their ability to renegotiate with creditor banks for early repayment of their debt at a discount. Together, the Alfa, Cydsa, Visa, and Vitro groups reduced their debt from $4.84 billion to $1.84 billion.

For example, in 1988 Alfa paid part of its debt in advance at a price below LIBOR, which resulted in a reduction of its bank liabilities in dollars by $982 million that year. Thus, that corporation's debt in dollars fell by 40 percent, totalling about $1.3 billion by the end of 1988.[14] Visa's debt was reduced by 67 percent from its 1982 level, dropping to $400 million, while Cydsa's debt dropped to $111 million when it obtained a 40 percent discount. By the end of December 1988, Vitro's debt came to $163 million, 78 percent less

---

[14]Before renegotiating its commitments with the banks, Alfa's debt had risen to more than U.S. $2.5 billion.

than its level in December 1982 (*El Norte*, March 3, 1989). Moreover, not only were they able to make payment on their debts; they also freed up large amounts of resources which were used immediately for important expansion and investment projects, including some abroad.

The case of Cemex exemplifies the new form of corporate expansion that followed after this period: with the purchase of Cementos Anáhuac in 1987, it developed a very aggressive growth program oriented toward winning not only the North American but the world cement market. In 1989 it acquired Cementos Tolteca (Tolmex), which made it equal in size to its main competitor in the United States and also increased its participation in the international market. Cemex estimates that its sales grew by more than 25 percent and its installed capacity by 38 percent.[15]

The Cemex experience also illustrates the close collaboration of the state in the Monterrey firms' reconversion process: the acquisition of Tolmex, which was owned by Blue Circle (a British company), required obtaining liquid resources on very short notice, since there was the risk that the company would fall into the hands of its foreign competitors. Government support was not long in coming: in 1989 the government, through the Comisión Nacional de Valores, authorized a loan of $157 million to Cemex (the largest loan ever authorized for a group of firms); at that time it represented 40 percent of the total amount loaned to private firms.

With the arrival of Carlos Salinas de Gortari to the presidency in 1989, the policies oriented toward economic opening took on a more defined direction, based on price stability and renegotiation of the external debt. The new policy sought to consolidate the process of trade opening by eliminating barriers and discretional restrictions to the free transit of goods in a rapid process of industrial and trade deregulation. Foreign investment was facilitated, particularly that channeled through Mexico's stock market. This latter measure especially benefited the Monterrey groups, since only eight groups in the entire country received the fruits of these investments in the first year. According to a study by Nacional Financiera (*El Universal*, May 12, 1990), Alfa was among these eight firms: it was able to capture 31.8 percent of the capital that entered Mexico through the stock market in 1990. Vitro and Cementos Mexicanos also appear, with lesser amounts.[16]

---

[15]As we shall see in the next chapter, Cemex has continued its process of expansion; in 1992 it acquired two important European cement firms, Valencia and Sansón.

[16]Other firms that benefited were Telmex, Cementos Apasco, Cifra, Peñoles, and Condumex.

While Miguel de la Madrid's policy tended to favor links with Latin America, Salinas promoted economic integration northward, carrying out a series of negotiations aimed at reaching a free trade agreement with the United States and forming a trade bloc to include Mexico, the United States, and Canada. The Monterrey businessmen claim that they tried to promote the idea of integration with the United States back in the de la Madrid period during direct conversations with the president, since the Latin American market presented increasing difficulties:

> They are countries that do not have hard currency to pay; they all have closed borders, except for Chile and now Mexico. To integrate with them is very hard. Furthermore, geography does not help. Products must be transported by sea with all the inconveniences and costs that this implies, while the United States and Canada are very close and have had open economies for a long time. They are used to allowing imports even of goods that they produce. The Latin American countries only import what is not produced in their territory (author interview with the general director of Imsa).

And, in fact, trade with those countries has declined from 6 percent in 1980 to approximately 3 percent in 1990.

Thus, businessmen perceived that there was an important change in the composition of the governing group with President Salinas's arrival to power: unlike earlier administrations, officials on the new team at the trade ministry accepted technical arguments while eliminating the "irrational prejudices" which in businessmen's opinion had given rise to absurd and unfair situations. These perceptions reflected the consolidation of the new alliance between business and government.

By the end of the 1980s, the large Monterrey firms had generally been able to overcome the crisis. In 1989, the combined debt of Alfa, Visa, Vitro, and Cydsa had been reduced by 62 percent compared to 1982 (*Expansión* 1989). Local corporations increased in size by more than 20 percent, and employment returned to the levels prevailing at the start of the decade. The strategy firms followed beginning in the mid-1980s to revitalize their economic situation was a combination of several things— from direct payments facilitated by FICORCA and the sale of firms up through capitalizations. That is, inviting creditors to trade in part of the debt for shares in the company (as in the case of Alfa and Visa).

The case of Alfa's recovery is very illustrative: in 1988 it ended a period of negotiations with creditor banks, reducing its liabilities by 60 percent compared to 1980. The group had given its creditors 45 percent of the company in exchange for the cancellation of part of its debt. In May 1989 it recovered these shares, returning control of its board of directors to Mexican hands, thereby eliminating the restrictions that the creditors had placed on the firm's strategic investments. Currently the total debt of the group is much less than shareholders' capital, in contrast with 1982 when liabilities were six times greater than shareholders' equity.

Visa, meanwhile, was able to end the decade larger than it was in 1980 thanks to the acquisition of Cervecería Moctezuma, which gave it 50 percent of the Mexican beer market. Prepayment of debt gave Vitro and Cydsa a good margin for growth: toward the end of 1989 Vitro had paid 60 percent of its debt with foreign banks, and its assets went over $2 billion beginning that year (*El Norte*, January 5, 1990). Cemex had eighteen plants producing 69 percent of cement exports to the United States by the end of the 1980s (*El Norte*, April 3, 1990).

The trade opening thus became the factor that from then on would define the domestic economic policy that aimed to reestablish Mexico's financial equilibrium. The country's private sector was divided with regard to the opening: all businessmen agreed that there was a need to increase productivity and competitiveness of Mexican products abroad. However, the firms tied to the domestic market continued to view Mexico's entry into the GATT, the accelerated deregulation of the external market, and the invasion of transnational productive capital with apprehension.

Because of this, firms which were somehow able to establish links to the export sector found themselves at an advantage vis-à-vis the new economic policy. Besides exporting, these firms followed a number of strategies such as partnerships with foreign firms and even transnationalization, as well as obtaining capital by placing shares on international stock markets. However, the new forms of insertion in world markets put an end to the advantages that the firms had enjoyed in the past in the protected Mexican market. This gave rise to a difficult period of adaptation to the conditions prevailing in international trade, as shall be seen in the next chapter.

4

Gaining Entry to International Markets

With the domestic crisis behind them, Monterrey Group firms accelerated their integration into international markets with aggressive investment and capitalization projects—with the backing of the state's new economic policy. This integration effort is taking place just as the production system worldwide is being restructured. The restructuring involves the whole set of industrial relations, from the production line to the reorganization of the firms' administrative structures. But it also includes a transformation in the forms of exchange and communication between firms. The features of an ever more globalized and competitive market demand new types of interfirm relationships. Partnerships, coinvestments, technology alliances, and supplier networks establish solid ties between industries, and these ties go beyond even the economic blocs themselves, shaping a truly worldwide network.

Monterrey Group firms have been tremendously successful in using these kinds of strategies and in a very short period have developed new kinds of ties with foreign firms all over the world, but especially in the United States. Partnerships and coinvestments with foreign firms had already been entered into as early as the 1960s by some firms of the Monterrey Group. This had enabled them to sell foreign products and receive technical assistance; in other words, these partnerships functioned as direct foreign investment. However, beginning in the 1980s, economic crisis and a drastic contraction of the domestic market, in addition to the policies of deregulation and economic opening, gave rise to a new kind of partnership which became the Monterrey firms' chief strategy for integrating into the world economy.

In the course of this process, the state continued to deepen the economic opening by eliminating obstacles to integration and giving resounding support to industries in expansion. It allowed foreign capital to hold a greater share in Mexican firms and made it easier for the latter to obtain a large part of the capital they needed to expand by issuing shares in the Mexican stock market.

To understand how large Mexican industry is integrating into the world economy, we must analyze both export developments and the different types of partnerships and coinvestments with foreign firms. Also, it is important to analyze the modernizing effect that the presence of foreign capital is having on Mexico through what are called supplier networks and technological alliances.

PRODUCING FOR EXPORT

The Salinas administration's policy for economic opening assumes the emergence of an export sector that can guarantee equilibrium in the balance of payments and the influx of foreign exchange needed for Mexico's industrial restructuring. And, indeed, exports grew by 32 percent between 1988 and 1990. However, economic opening also led to an increase in imports, which upset Mexico's balance of payments; by the end of 1991 Mexico's trade deficit had increased 270 percent, for a negative trade balance of $11.182 billion, compared to $3.25 billion in 1990 (INEGI 1992). In 1991 imports grew by 28.7 percent, reaching a total of $38.357 billion, while exports increased barely 1.5 percent, reaching $27.175 billion.[17]

This situation, which a few years earlier would have sufficed to touch off a new crisis, was eased somewhat by direct foreign investment of nearly $33.167 billion in 1988–91. Of this amount, $9.897 billion entered Mexico in 1991 alone (SECOFI 1992).

Most of this investment was channeled through the Mexican stock exchange. Although close to 60 percent of investment went to the industrial sector (see figure 2), there is an ongoing debate in Mexico as to whether it is sufficiently secure and stable to continue financing the country's growing current account deficit in the future, given the natural instability of stock market investments. Nevertheless, according to Mexico's trade ministry, imports of capital goods grew by 40 percent in 1991, totaling close to $12 billion. This means that a part of imports have been used for industrial modernization (*La Jornada*, January 13, 1992).

---

[17]The slowdown in export growth is largely related to the drop in oil prices.

Figure 2
Direct Foreign Investment by Sector
(as of September 1991)

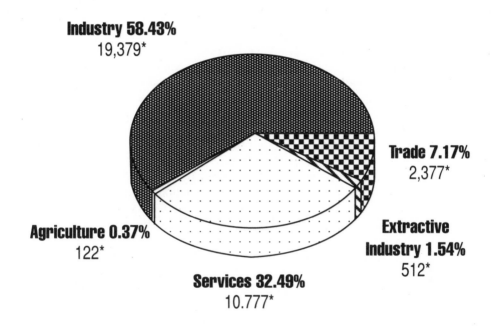

Industry 58.43%
19,379*

Trade 7.17%
2,377*

Agriculture 0.37%
122*

Extractive
Industry 1.54%
512*

Services 32.49%
10.777*

* Millions of dollars.

Source: SECOFI

Together with other economic indicators[18] these figures seem to point to the success of Salinas's policy of economic opening. However, it is important to emphasize that these results do not rest on the strict implementation of an orthodox neoliberal policy, since the controls exercised by the state over a significant number of economic variables—such as price and wage controls,[19] an exchange rate freeze,[20] and keeping interests rates high—are far from a free play of market forces and a situation of nonintervention in the economy. These and other government actions explicitly support firms linked to the export sector. It is too early to analyze whether this support will yield results sufficient to offset the high social cost that workers and the nonexport sector have had to pay, above all with regard to plant closures,[21] deteriorating wages (see figure 1), and deepening social inequality due to the extremely high concentration of capital that this development model fosters. I venture no predictions on the favored firms' ability to compete internationally once the ability of the state to control the aforementioned variables is hampered by further opening, nor regarding the solidity and permanence of the 64 percent of foreign investment that is channeled through the Mexican stock market. What is important is that state support fulfilled its objectives by rescuing leading industrial groups, which were then able to reorient their production toward export markets.

Some of the firms studied joined the ranks of major Latin American exporters, alongside the transnational firms in Mexico's auto industry. For example, in 1990 Alfa and Vitro were ninth and eighteenth, respectively, among the top exporter firms in Latin America (*Progreso* 1991). Indeed, that year ten of the top twenty Latin American exporter firms were Mexican. Alfa's 1990 exports were $520 million, close to 20 percent of the total value of its sales that year (see table 2). Likewise, Vitro exported 20 percent of its

[18]Official statistics for 1991: GDP growth of 3.6 percent; an increase in private consumption of 5 percent in real terms, i.e., double the rate of population growth; a 13 percent increase in private investment; a decrease of 7 percent in public investment (report from the Sistema Nacional de Cuentas Nacionales and INEGI, March 9, 1992).

[19]During the concertation among the state, business, and labor that took place in the framework of the Pact for Stability and Economic Growth (PECE) in November 1991, the three parties reached agreement to increase wages by no more than 11.5 percent.

[20]According to a report in the daily newspaper *El Financiero* (January 31, 1992), overvaluation of the peso reached 11.7 percent in December 1991, due to a 50 percent reduction in the daily slide of the peso as agreed to in the PECE.

[21]Jaime Salcedo, chairman of the National Chamber of Manufacturers (CANA-CINTRA), notes that six hundred small industries closed during 1991. Many of them were displaced by foreign companies or by large industrial consortiums (*El Financiero*, January 31, 1992).

total 1990 sales, or about \$311 million.[22] This figure contrasts with Vitro's exports in 1980 (less that \$38 million), and it gives us an idea of the significant turn in the firm's orientation toward foreign markets (*El Norte*, November 19, 1991).

Cydsa's exports grew spectacularly during the 1980s; by 1988 they were close to \$117 million per year and by 1990 nearly \$200 million, that is, almost 24 percent of sales. Currently, some of its plants have export rates as high as 30 percent, as in the case of Derivados Acrílicos, in San Luis Potosí, which exports to eighteen countries (only 14 percent of its exports are to the United States). Crysel, a subsidiary in Guadalajara, exports 25 percent of its total production (*El Norte*, November 19 and 20, 1991). Other large Mexican exporters in 1990 were Cemex and Imsa, who exported close to \$106 and \$102 million, respectively.

However, this rapid export growth slowed in 1991, when there was a sharp drop in foreign sales for most Monterrey firms. Exports of the main Monterrey firms contracted by 10.7 percent compared to 1990, according to the Bolsa Mexicana de Valores. Cemex's 1991 exports fell 43 percent;[23] Imsa's fell 15.8 percent; Alfa dropped 13.9 percent; Vitro's fell 7.2 percent; and Cydsa's exports declined 0.6 percent. Among the firms studied, only the Visa group increased its exports, by 1 percent (see table 3). Although the

TABLE 3
VALUE OF EXPORTS FROM 1990 TO 1991
(IN MILLIONS OF DOLLARS)

Group	Exports in 1991	Exports as % of Sales	Real Change 1990–1991
Alfa	382.14	16.9%	− 13.9%
Cemex	53.94	3.4%	− 43.4%
Cydsa	169.50	23.5%	− 0.6%
Imsa	78.03	11.6%	− 15.8%
Vitro	246.39	8.8%	− 7.2%
Visa	55.41	3.1%	1.0%

Source: Bolsa Mexicana de Valores.

importance of this reduction cannot be determined based on data from one year alone, the drop in exports may be due to a number of factors: the U.S. recession, the recovery of Mexico's domestic market, and market and intrafirm adjustments. Further, efforts to

---

[22]Calculated from data in table 2, converting from 1990 pesos.

[23]In the case of Cemex, the drastic reduction is largely due to the duty imposed on its exports when it lost a dumping suit in the United States.

control inflation have led to overvaluation of the Mexican peso, lessening the competitiveness of Mexican exports abroad. But along with these factors which inhibited the participation of Mexican products in the international market, Mexican exporters came up against all kinds of protectionist measures—mainly in the U.S. market, as we shall see in the next section.

OBSTACLES TO TRADE WITH THE UNITED STATES

The policy of trade opening toward the north occurred at a disadvantageous time for Mexico due to the dependence of the Mexican economy on the U.S. economy. Although only 6 percent of the United States' foreign trade was with Mexico in 1988, 60 percent of Mexico's exports and 65 percent of its imports were with the United States (Destler 1992). Alongside this asymmetry, Mexico decided to reorient its economy toward the world market at one of the most competitive moments in its history. Mexico's trade opening is being pushed in an era when neoprotectionism is the rule and sanitary norms and other trade controls proliferate. Such unfavorable conditions make it essential that Mexico not only sign the North American Free Trade Agreement, but also that it achieve the best possible conditions. Lowering defenses by reducing tariffs and promoting foreign investment without establishing effective protection mechanisms at least parallel to those that Mexican products face abroad runs the risk of losing control over mechanisms of the domestic economy, subordinating it to the fluctuations and interests that dominate the world economy and oligopolistic international markets. Furthermore, the benefits of international trade have historically tended to concentrate disproportionately in the advanced countries, while the number of undeveloped countries that have shared these benefits has been quite small.

Since the industries under discussion channeled a large part of their production abroad before NAFTA, they have had to operate under restrictive measures established unilaterally by U.S. trade authorities. In this sense, the experiences of the Monterrey Group firms constitute an interesting experiment regarding the conditions of economic opening: controlled markets, antidumping suits, phytosanitary regulations, embargoes, and high tariffs on many products.

The restrictions that controlled markets still place on steel products exporters exemplify these difficulties. Some of the firms studied came up against this barrier when they exported galvanized sheet metal, painted steel, panels, etc. Beginning in 1985, their exports came under a quota system which initially granted Mexican steel producers only 0.2 percent of the U.S. steel market.

Negotiations between the two governments freed Mexican products from a compensatory tax as long as Mexico agreed to limit its exports. From that moment on, in order to obtain export permits, steel industrialists had to negotiate with the U.S. government, which verified that the exported tons did not exceed the U.S. quota.

In response, the industrialists developed all kinds of strategies to increase their exports. One of them explained:

> Brazil is the main producer of steel plate in Latin America. However, it does not produce galvanized steel. Therefore, we signed an agreement to bring close to 15,000 tons of Brazilian steel to Mexico per month for a year. We galvanized it here and exported it to the United States with a Brazilian certificate of origin. We were able to do this for just one year; then they caught on (author interview, June 1990).

Through its trade ministry and in cooperation with the Business Chamber of steel industrialists, the Mexican government has been negotiating changes in the quota system with U.S. authorities. However, according to Mexican steel producers, as long as there is no trade agreement in place that grants benefits similar to those won by Canada (it became the main exporter of steel to the United States when freed from the quota system), Mexican steel will not have a guaranteed market.

Besides controlled markets, exporting firms also face anti-dumping suits or charges of unfair trade practices. All of the groups studied have been subjected to these kinds of suits. Imsa, for example, was accused of dumping in connection with a project to export batteries even before actual export began. Vitro faced a similar charge in its exports of porcelain-enameled steel, while its cut crystal products have been hit with a much higher tariff than that set by Mexico for imports of the same product. Vitro is also facing the threat of an antidumping suit for exports of flat glass to the United States.

However, the best-known dumping case is that of Cementos Mexicanos. The problem began on September 29, 1989, when six U.S. cement producers accused Cemex of dumping its product or covertly subsidizing its sales to the United States. This came after Mexican cement exports had gained 14 percent of the market in three U.S. border states (Arizona, New Mexico, and Texas) and climbed to $111 million (*El Norte*, July 17, 1990). The International Trade Commission (ITC) issued a temporary ruling in which it determined that damage to the U.S. cement industry could be presumed since Cemex was selling at a price that was 51–57 percent below its selling price in Mexico; the ruling would not be final until the plaintiff firms provided the necessary proof of harm. If the accusation were proven, the U.S. government could tax Cemex imports to make them comparable in price to cement from U.S. firms (*El Norte*, April 6, 1990). On August 13, the ITC ruled against Cemex, slapping a compensatory tax of 58 percent on the firm's cement exports to the United States. Backed by the Mexican government, Cemex immediately appealed the ruling to the U.S. International Trade Court and to GATT authorities in Geneva. The effect of the trade sanction was reflected in Cemex's sales abroad: at the start of 1992 Cemex reported a 30 percent drop in its exports, representing close to 1.2 million tons (*Notimex*, February 26, 1992). The recovery of the Mexican construction industry and Cemex's diversification into other expanding sectors, such as tourism, compensated for losses due to reduced exports.

According to some business leaders interviewed, Mexico lacks the experience and aggressiveness required to respond in kind to U.S. protectionism. Although it has a law against unfair trade practices, the law's implementation is still very ineffective, above all because follow-through on a case of this kind requires that Mexican authorities send specialists abroad to investigate the validity of the accusations, which is a lengthy and costly process.

BUSINESSMEN AND NAFTA

Considering the tariff and nontariff barriers that Mexican products come up against in their trade with the United States, businessmen view the signing of NAFTA as indispensable. In November 1990 the first meeting took place between the presidents of Mexico and the United States to launch negotiations on the trade agreement. Monterrey was selected as the site of this meeting, and Monterrey businessmen took the opportunity to express their main concerns and expectations regarding NAFTA. Some of the topics they raised were the development of mechanisms to resolve trade conflicts, the elimination of nontariff barriers, recognition of the asymmetry between the two economies, restrictions on the entry of foreign banking into Mexico, and equalization of the fiscal system. These concerns were voiced in a published document entitled *Cumbre 90*.

TRADE CONFLICTS AND NONTARIFF BARRIERS

The issues of nontariff barriers and trade conflicts are of crucial interest to Monterrey businessmen. Because firms are powerless to resolve problems in these areas on their own, they expect the Mexican government to intervene. Although the businessmen believe that a trade agreement will not eliminate all dumping charges, for example, they expect that trade disputes or disagreements will be resolved in a tribunal comprising Mexican and American members, and a third party when necessary to assure impartial rulings. Under present conditions, an American judge decides cases unilaterally and applies penalties. Further, some businessmen believe that NAFTA may be too general, allowing the United States the opportunity to get around general agreements in order to protect U.S. firms from competition (*El Norte*, June 14, 1990).

Moreover, Monterrey businessmen think that the Mexican market is now more open than the U.S. market. Indeed, due to U.S. compensatory measures, Mexico's policy of supporting and promoting investment and exports underwent significant modifications that eliminated all the direct benefits that litigants in dumping cases could claim were subsidies. The Mexican government also gradually eliminated import permit requirements and left tariffs as the sole means to control imports. In other words, Mexico opened its borders with the aim of fostering foreign investment without having negotiated more favorable conditions for its products abroad.

The Monterrey businessmen's position with regard to U.S. protectionism is summed up by Cemex's general director, Lorenzo Zambrano:

> There is not the slightest doubt that the United States has an extraordinary record in terms of opening markets. . . . However, in recent years U.S. trade policy has kept the same liberal facade although in reality it has changed noticeably. . . . Our advances on what the Americans themselves have prescribed as the road to success have brought us up against unsurmountable barriers whose only purpose is to protect less efficient and less competitive producers within the United States (Zambrano 1990).

ASYMMETRY AND THE FINANCIAL SECTOR

Another issue of great interest to Monterrey businessmen is that the United States recognize the asymmetry that exists between the two countries as they prepare to sign NAFTA. Rafael Páez, general director of Alfa, summed up their position: "The Agreement must take into consideration the differences between the two countries and allow for less aggressive tariff reductions on Mexico's part than reductions carried out between the United States and Canada" (Páez 1990). This concern is related, on the one hand, to the need to give Mexican manufacturing firms time to gain strength and prepare to face external competition and, on the other, to the goal of protecting the country's financial sector. In the latter case, businessmen are reacting to U.S. moves to gain access to financial services in Mexico. Othón Ruiz-Montemayor, general director of Visa (which recently acquired one of the largest banks in Mexico), summarized this concern:

> The experience of other countries points to the risks of abruptly exposing national financial inter-mediaries to external competition without first giving them the opportunity to consolidate, mod-ernize, and function in an atmosphere of competi-tion. The risk here is that national intermediaries could be displaced by foreign ones (Ruiz-Mon-temayor 1990).

The fact that U.S. negotiators agreed to grant Mexican banks a ten-year period before bringing U.S. financial services to Mexican territory, as well as the recent reprivatization of Mexican banks nationalized in 1982, attest to the pressure exerted by Mexican businessmen to keep banking services in national hands. In fact, four of the ten banks reprivatized by the end of January 1992 were acquired by groups of investors mostly from Monterrey. This is the case with BANCOMER, the second-largest banking institution in Mexico, which was acquired by Vamsa, the financial arm of the Visa group controlled by Eugenio Garza Lagüera. Also, the SERFIN bank, which was owned by the Garza Sada family before it was expropriated, has now returned to the group through Adrián Sada, the main stockholder in Vitro, and Javier Garza Sepúlveda of the Gentor Group.[24] Through these operations, Mon-terrey businessmen and investors have been able to acquire control of 41.8 percent of the Mexican banking system's assets—a total investment of approximately $3.8 billion (*El Norte*, January 27, 1992). Thus, the arrangement that had prevailed in Monterrey for decades, based on the integration of industrial and financial capital

---

[24]The other banks bought by Monterrey groups are: Banca Confía, acquired by the Abaco group led by Jorge Lankenau, and the Banco del Oriente, acquired by the Margen group of Marcelo and Ricardo Margáin.

but interrupted by the expropriation of the banks, has reappeared.[25]

According to Monterrey businessmen, direct U.S. participation might destabilize the process of restructuring the financial system; time must be allowed for the transformation of Mexico's financial structure and for the equalization of service conditions:

> Although tremendous progress has recently been made in financial matters, high interest rates persist due both to the risk perceived in our currency and to the high costs of intermediation, and even to an inadequate term structure. Our savings are basically short term, and there is very little depth and stability in our capital market (Ruiz-Montemayor 1990).

FISCAL MECHANISMS

According to Monterrey businessmen, another disadvantage when facing foreign competition has to do with the tax system. In their opinion, the Mexican government must increase its revenues by broadening the tax base and reducing taxes on firms to their level in the United States. "We need fiscal coordination mechanisms between both countries in order to avoid putting Mexican firms at a disadvantage vis-à-vis U.S. firms" (Kalifa 1990). Lastly, the businessmen demand a stable real exchange rate, since this is important when planning a firm's development, as the general director and chairman of the Imsa management board, Eugenio Clariond Reyes, noted: "We do not want an undervaluation that subsidizes, we want stable real parity" (Clariond Reyes 1990).

As a result, Monterrey businessmen want adequate periods stipulated in NAFTA to allow time for Mexico to reduce the existing asymmetry, particularly in light of the international and U.S. recessions. The director of Alfa expressed these concerns clearly:

> Mexican imports of intermediate and consumer goods have grown steadily by 40 percent per year over the last three years. This, together with the recessionary international environment, would produce even greater aggressiveness on the part of foreign competitors in the Mexican market and possibly put our work force at risk. Therefore, it is

---

[25]Before the expropriation, Visa controlled 77.8 percent of the capital of SERFIN, while Vitro controlled 81 percent of BANPAIS (CIEN 1983).

> urgent that we define our industries' competitive
> position. . . . It would be important to evaluate
> those Mexican industries that have intrinsic strate-
> gic viability and then carry out skillful negotia-
> tions to avoid dispossessing them as a result of an
> overly aggressive process (Páez 1990).

In other words, Páez proposes an in-depth analysis of Mexico's
industries, not in order to protect the weakest firms but to give
those with competitive potential time to grow stronger.

FREEING PRICES

Something else that the private sector pointed out to the Mexican
government was the impossibility of concluding and signing
NAFTA without first freeing prices. In recent years, the big Monterrey consortia have resented the price controls they had agreed
on with the government, since their profits have been constantly
reduced despite an increase in sales volume. Also, price controls
can constitute a disadvantage when facing foreign competitors
who can sell their products at whatever price they choose. In this
regard, Monterrey businessmen noted:

> Despite the fact that the government has made
> progress in deregulating the domestic economy,
> price controls translate into unequal conditions
> when facing international competitors (Zambrano
> 1990).

And:

> In the medium term, free trade abroad is not
> possible without free trade at home. We know that
> in the short term there is structural inflation which
> prevents totally freeing prices. Nevertheless, we
> believe that this is one of the conditions that must
> be met if we are to compete successfully in inter-
> national markets (Ruiz-Montemayor 1990).

Negotiating the trade agreement proved to be much harder
than the Mexican government had expected. U.S. sectors opposed
to the treaty gained strength over the course of the 1992 presidential campaign. The pressure they exerted reinforced the demands
of the U.S. negotiators, who hoped to gain support in Congress by
winning key concessions from Mexico. In March 1992, the head of

the U.S. Department of Energy told the press that an important step had been taken toward the total liberalization of the energy and petrochemical market. Meanwhile, the Mexican Ministry of Commerce and Industrial Development (SECOFI) acknowledged that it had accepted the U.S. proposal to modify foreign investment legislation and implement a reclassification of basic petrochemicals in order to allow participation of foreign capital in that industry. The limit to the share that U.S. financial institutions could hold in Mexican banks was raised from 10 to 15 percent, and some concessions were made in the automobile sector (*La Jornada*, March 13, 1992; *El Financiero*, March 13, 1992).

Mexico, on the other hand, has encountered serious difficulties in winning concessions. It had no success in one area of crucial interest to the Monterrey Group industrialists: the Mexican negotiators proposed that a trilateral tribunal be established to deal with nonjudicial matters such as trade conflicts, but the proposal was rejected.

While the mere expectation of signing the agreement has accelerated the integration process, the Monterrey businessmen's opinion is that the lack of reciprocity in trade measures cost Mexico $8 billion in 1991.[26] Aside from the unequal distribution of the potential benefits of such an agreement within Mexico, the problem of asymmetry between the two countries puts Mexico at a disadvantage in the negotiations, and this fact may have consequences which we cannot yet foresee.

PARTNERSHIPS AND COINVESTMENTS

While negotiations for signing NAFTA continued, Monterrey firms pursued integration into international markets along various lines. Besides exports, the Monterrey groups used mechanisms such as partnerships and coinvestments with foreign firms, primarily from the United States. The forms of partnership that have developed are myriad and to various degrees involve changes in the composition of capital within the respective firm. Partnerships may mean a simple exchange of shares, which allows both partners to use marketing channels in the other country, or it may include joint founding of a new firm and construction of a new plant; the advantage in the latter case is that the plant becomes a customer or a supplier of subsidiaries of the corporations in the partnership.

The case of Vitro is the best example for demonstrating the features of this process, since it has had partnerships with foreign

---

[26]Statement by a group of Mexican businessmen to Treasury Secretary Pedro Aspe during a meeting at the Center for U.S.-Mexican Studies, University of California, San Diego, February 1992.

firms since 1965 (when it entered into an association with Pilkington PLC). In the 1980s, Vitro carried out coinvestments with
Ford and Samsonite, among others, but the case that is of interest
here is its partnership with Whirlpool. In 1987 Vitro sold Whirlpool 49 percent of the shares in Vitromatic, one of its subsidiaries
producing electrical appliances. This transaction resulted in the
construction of the Acros industrial complex, which gave Vitro
access to its new partner's technology as well as the possibility to
manufacture and sell a greater number of products, such as Acros,
Supermatic, Crolls, and Whirlpool, among others. In effect, this
kind of operation is a form of direct foreign investment, but in
association with a Mexican firm. The plant is established in Mexico, so the foreign firm gains marketing channels there and a share
of the profits, while the Mexican firm gains technology, capital,
and the possibility to manufacture and sell certain products with
foreign trademarks. As Ernesto Martens, general director of Vitro,
put it:

> The investment in Whirlpool is economically justi-
> fied because Vitromatic makes products that are
> needed in Mexico and can be economically pro-
> duced domestically because of the large market.
> Through Vitromatic, Vitro can sell Whirlpool
> products at competitive costs, as well as distribute
> imported products that are needed here, but not
> in numbers that justify local manufacturing (*El
> Financiero Internacional*, April 6, 1992).

Another interesting form of association was carried out by
Vitro in 1991 with the U.S. firm Corning: through this operation
Corning acquired 49 percent of Vitro's stock, but at the same time
Vitro acquired 49 percent of the U.S. firm's shares, which gives it
maximum return on its investment and the benefits of a global
position. With this partnership, Vitro has gained production facili-
ties in Canada, England, France, Germany, Italy, and Brazil (although Vitro has had commercial and production activities in the
latter for years) (*El Financiero Internacional*, April 6, 1992). This kind
of partnership is a double joint venture, in which the advantage is
that the firms' products and processes are complementary. Corning is strong in glass-making and fusion technologies, while
Vitro's strengths are in processing, treatment, and decorating
technologies, as well as machinery. In terms of distribution, Vitro
is strong in the Middle East; Corning is powerful in Germany and
France.

Figure 3
Vitro's Ties to Foreign Firms

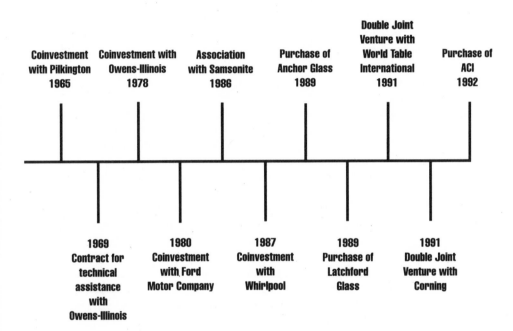

Coinvestment with Pilkington 1965

Coinvestment with Owens-Illinois 1978

Association with Samsonite 1986

Purchase of Anchor Glass 1989

Double Joint Venture with World Table International 1991

Purchase of ACI 1992

1969 Contract for technical assistance with Owens-Illinois

1980 Coinvestment with Ford Motor Company

1987 Coinvestment with Whirlpool

1989 Purchase of Latchford Glass

1991 Double Joint Venture with Corning

Vitro also has other U.S. partners, such as Owens-Illinois and the American Silver Company (see figure 3) for the production, marketing, and distribution of its products, not to mention the technological advantages that these partnerships bring (*Expansión* 1992a).

Alfa, for its part, has formed alliances with Dravo, BASF, DuPont, Metecno, Ford, Stone Container, Kawasaki, Akzo, Man Gbh, Amoco, Himont, and Teksid (see table 4). Its association with Himont, which began in 1989, resulted in the creation of Indelpro in Mexico. Alfa invested close to $100 million in the new firm and gained control of 70 percent of the shares. Indelpro produces polypropylene (used in packing material), film, autoparts, electrical appliances, sacks, and a wide range of plastics, all of which were previously imported into Mexico. The firm will gain a market of close to $100 million. Furthermore, the fact that Himont is a technology leader in its field means that its partnership with Alfa introduces new technology in Mexico via the new plant and guarantees the international competitiveness of the products.

In general, the main products Alfa sells abroad are aluminum cylinder heads, synthetic fibers, steel, and carpets. Most of these products are manufactured through coinvestments with multinational firms such as Ford, Fiat, and Stone Container. For example, in 1980, Alfa created Nemak in partnership with Ford Motor Company; the firm now produces aluminum cylinder heads for Ford, Chrysler, General Motors, and Renault in the United States.

From the point of view of foreign capital, the search for Mexican partners seems to be driven not only by an interest in getting products into the Mexican market, but also in building a production platform from which foreign firms can launch into the rapidly growing Latin American market (and/or the U.S. market, in the case of some European and Japanese firms, in anticipation of NAFTA). The need to get geographically closer to these markets grows stronger under the new schemes for production organization; just-in-time production (JIT) demands closer proximity to suppliers and customers. Distance differences in transportation costs and delivery times are frequently the determining factor in a product's competitiveness.

Along these lines, it is interesting to note that new plants that result from coinvestments generally are built on Mexican territory. This is the case with Nemak, the Alfa subsidiary created through a coinvestment with Ford, and Galvamet, another subsidiary founded with Metecno, an Italian partner (*El Norte*, January 30, 1992).

The interest in partnerships with Monterrey companies comes not only from the United States but also from Europe. For example,

TABLE 4
SOME ASSOCIATIONS OF THE MONTERREY FIRMS

Corporation	Firm	Foreign Partner	Year	Features of the Association
Alfa		Ford (USA)	1979	Creation of the Nemak Plant
		Himont (Italy)	1989	Creation of the Indelpro Plant
	Nemak	Teksid (Italy)	1989	Share of Stock & Technological Alliance
		Metecno (Italy)	1992	Creation of Galvamet Plant
		Kawasaki (Japan)		Association to Manufacture some Products
		Fiat (Italy)		Association to Manufacture Autoparts
Vitro	Vitro Plan	Pilkington (UK)	1965	Association to Manufacture Floated Glass & Technological Alliance
	Enseres Domésticos	Owens-Illinois (USA)	1969	Technical Assistance Contract
	Enseres Domésticos	Owens-Illinois (USA)	1978	Partnership and Marketing
	Vitro Plan	Ford (USA)	1980	Association to Manufacture Automotive Glass
		Samsonite (USA)	1986	Association to Manufacture Luggage and Furniture
	Vitromatic	Whirlpool (USA)	1987	Creation of Industrial Complex; Reciprocal Distribution Agreement
	Vitro Envases	Anchor Glass (USA)	1989	Vitro Acquires the Firm
	Vitro Envases	Latchford Glass (USA)	1989	Vitro Acquires the Firm
	Vitro Crisa	World Tableware International (USA)	1991	Vitro Acquires 49% of WTI's Amsilco Division; WTI Acquires 49% of Vitrocrisa Division
	Vitro Crisa	Corning (USA)	1991	Vitro Acquires 49% of Corning's Table & Kitchen Ware; Corning Acquires 49% of Vitro Corning
	Vitro Plan	ACI America (UK)	1992	Vitro Acquires the Firm
Cemex		Gulf Coast Portland Cement (USA)	1989	Cemex Acquires the Firm
		Houston Shell and Concrete (USA)	1989	Cemex Acquires the Firm
		Southwestern Sunbelt Cement (USA)	1989	Cemex Acquires the Firm
		Sunward Materials USA	1989	Cemex Acquires the Firm
		Pacific Coast Cement	1990	Cemex Acquires the Firm
		C.L. Pharris (USA)	1992	Cemex Acquires the Firm
		Valencia (Spain)	1992	Cemex Acquires the Firm
		Sanson (Spain)	1992	Cemex Acquires the Firm
Cydsa		Rayon Yarn Corp		Cydsa Acquires the Firm

the Belgian firm ITS Fabry offered Cydsa a partnership in May 1992 to market Cydsa's products in Europe. ITS has customs, transportation, storage, and fiduciary services, and operates in the twelve countries of the European Community. The company was attracted by Cydsa's coverage in exporting acrylic fiber to twenty-five countries (*El Norte*, May 15, 1992).

One of the fundamental criteria guiding the Monterrey firms' choice of foreign partners is product complementarity. Practically all new plant construction resulting from coinvestments with foreign partners is located in the vicinity of subsidiaries of the Mexican companies which can become suppliers or customers of the new plant. Thus, for example, the new plastics factory Alfa will build in association with Eastman Chemical, a Kodak subsidiary, will be located in the vicinity of Petrocel and Tereftalatos, other Alfa-owned plants. They manufacture inputs that the new firm will need to produce two-liter plastic soda bottles, a package size new to Mexico and Latin America. Thus Alfa gains a customer for some of its products (*El Norte*, May 8, 1992).

Several corporations are also pursuing partnerships that enhance vertical integration, confirming our observation that companies have abandoned the indiscriminate diversification they carried out in the 1970s.

TRANSNATIONALIZATION

Businesses' efforts to gain entry to international markets are not limited to associations or partnerships. The largest Monterrey corporations have begun to expand abroad by purchasing or constructing firms in other countries. The most spectacular cases are those of Vitro and Cemex, who have been acquiring U.S. firms. Vitro had held shares in Anchor Glass Container, based in Tampa, Florida, since 1983. In August 1989, the group implemented a strategy to take control of that firm by buying up a large portion of stock at $20 per share, more than twice its market value. Anchor's board of directors was firmly opposed to Vitro's takeover bid and tried to block it. Vitro prevailed after a costly, two-month legal battle, agreeing to pay $21.50 per Anchor share and to withdraw the suit it had filed against the U.S. firm's chief executives. Vincent J. Naimoli, chairman of the board and chief executive at Anchor, was replaced by Ernesto Martens of Vitro in both posts (*El Norte*, October 14, 1989). Anchor Glass is the second-largest container company in the United States, and it is 307th among the 500 largest firms in the country (*Fortune*, April 20, 1992). Its acquisition gave Vitro a dominant position with a 25 percent share of the U.S. glass container market (*El Financiero Internacional*, April 6, 1992). Furthermore, the purchase of Anchor put Vitro third worldwide as a glass producer, after the U.S. firm Owens-Illinois and the French firm Saint Gobien. Meanwhile, Vitro management has proved beneficial for Anchor. Under its Mexican directors the U.S. firm went from losses of $34.5 million in 1989 (the year it was bought) to $18 million in profits in the first nine months of 1991 (*América Economía*, November 1991). Anchor's sales grew 1.2 percent that year despite the recession.

Later in 1991, Vitro also acquired Latchford Glass. With these acquisitions, over half of Vitro's income was coming from outside of Mexico. To consolidate its position in the United States, in May 1992 Vitro bought yet another firm, ACI (America, Inc.), with 120 glass processing plants and wholesale and retail sales offices (*El Porvenir*, May 20, 1992).[27]

Cemex, meanwhile, first globalized through exports, using the marketing channels of the Mexican cement firms it acquired during the 1980s and early 1990s. When it bought Cementos Anáhuac in 1987, it entered markets on the Gulf of Mexico, mainly in Florida and the Caribbean. In 1990 it acquired Cementos Tolteca, which gave it entry to the market of the southwestern United States (California and Arizona) through an association with Blue Circle West in the production of premixed concrete and in cement distribution.

Toward the end of the 1980s, Cemex decided to expand further by buying cement plants in the United States. In 1989 it acquired four U.S. cement producing firms and one marketing firm with outlets in Casas Grandes and Phoenix, Arizona; El Paso, Texas; Albuquerque, New Mexico; and El Centro and National City, California. In September 1989 it bought Gulf Coast Portland Cement, the largest cement producer in Houston, and Houston Shell and Concrete, which has forty processing plants. These two firms became part of Southwestern Sunbelt (SSC), a consortium previously owned in equal parts by Cemex and Southdown Cement (the second-largest cement producer in the United States). After Cemex's acquisitions of operations in Houston, Southdown decided to sell Cemex its share in the consortium. In a press release in Houston, Southdown reported: "A Cemex affiliate will indirectly acquire 50 percent of the capital of SSC, giving the Mexican firm 100 percent ownership of SSC" (*El Norte*, September 6, 1989). With these operations Cemex had consolidated as the main cement supplier in west Texas, southern California, and New Mexico. Cemex later acquired Pacific Coast Cement and C.L. Pharris in Los

---

[27] ACI is located in Tennessee; the firm used to be part of BTR-Nylex, an Australian company, which in turn is owned by BTR-PLC, a British firm. Vitro acquired 100 percent of the stock through its Vitro Plano division.

Angeles, California. Finally, in 1992 Cemex took a leap in its transnationalization when it gained a position in Europe by purchasing two large Spanish firms, La Valenciana and Sansón (*Expansión* 1992b).

The capital that the Monterrey firms needed to carry forward their expansion and modernization projects was obtained largely in international capital markets. Vitro and Cemex implemented a successful financial strategy in which they (along with Teléfonos de México) were able to place large numbers of shares on the European and New York stock markets. Cemex, for example, obtained close to $600 million in April 1992, after placing 37 percent of its offering in the United States, 39 percent in Europe, and the remaining 24 percent in Mexico.[28] This was the second-largest international stock offering ever by a Mexican private firm (*El Norte*, April 15, 1992). The Mexican firms' success in the stock markets has to do with the international interest in investing in oligopolistic firms with broad control over rapidly growing national markets (such as the construction industry, beer, etc.), because of the high and stable returns which this type of operation can guarantee.

However, Vitro's and Cemex's incursions into the big leagues of industrial production have not been problem free. The advantage that the Monterrey corporations initially offered investors seemed to vanish when the firms transnationalized. Paradoxically, just as Cemex was winning an important position in the European market, its European acquisitions were upsetting its U.S. and European investors, leading to a 25 percent drop in the value of Cemex shares over a three-month period. Market analysts in the United States observed that investors had put money in a firm oriented toward a domestic market with an estimated growth rate of 10 percent for 1992; what they got was a firm with big expansion ambitions, and this eliminated its attractive "Mexicanness."[29] In the view of investors, the acquisition of the Spanish firms, which faced a more competitive and slow growth market, would dilute Cemex's advantage by including their performance in the firm's total accounts. As an international firm, Cemex shares would move toward the price level of U.S. and European cement stocks. While Mexico shares tend to sell at close to 30 percent above market value, shares of foreign cement producers generally sell at 20 or 30 percent below their respective market value.

---

[28]The stock placement was made up of an offering of 12.5 million American depository shares and 8 million common stock certificates.

[29]Analysts from the firms of Oppenheimer, Goldman Sachs, H.G. Wellington, and Arnold & S. Bleichroeder.

Vitro's shares displayed a similar pattern following the firm's aggressive expansion at the end of the 1980s.[30] In pursuing its transnationalization process the corporation sacrificed profits, which dropped 19.4 percent in real terms from 1990 to 1991. Also, with its purchase of Anchor Glass, Vitro entered a depressed U.S. market, further diminishing its profits and the value of its shares.

These cases lead to some interesting inferences. First, they show that investors and firms abroad view Mexico as an attractive, growing market. Second, the oligopolistic features of the large Mexican firms, some of which control more than 50 percent of the national market for their respective products, offer an initial advantage—the ability to use stock market capital abroad to finance reconversion and expansion projects. However, this advantage ends with the entry of foreign competition and/or the transnationalization of the Mexican firms themselves, which in the future will have to compete on an equal footing with foreign giants.

Cemex's strategy seems to reflect its awareness of the temporary nature of its advantage in the Mexican market. Its strongest competitor, Holderbank of Switzerland, the world's leading cement producer, already has a 60 percent share in Apasco, the second-largest cement producer in Mexico. For the time being, Cemex has a greater cash flow than it can spend in its domestic market, even with projected yearly capital investments of $400 million through 1996, since it will generate nearly $900 million in excess cash over the next four years (*El Norte*, July 29, 1992). For these reasons the firm is using its current advantages to grow and become stronger in foreign markets. At the same time, Europe offers Cemex an alternative to the U.S. market, where a high countervailing duty was applied to its product after the company lost a dumping suit; this hindered its ability to supply the concrete producers it owns in the United States, and the latter had to recur to U.S. suppliers.

The advantages and disadvantages of the strategies adopted by Monterrey Group companies may change in the future as economic opening and integration to the U.S. economy advance. The complete liberalization of imports and the establishment of completely U.S.-owned firms in Mexico are real threats to the stability and even the survival of Mexican industries. However, modernization is already under way within the firms themselves through a new type of relationship between customers and suppliers and through technological changes.

---

[30]In 1991, Vitro invested U.S. $368 million, 24 percent more than in 1990, according to the firm's director (*El Norte*, April 6, 1992). In November 1991 it placed 9 million shares on the stock markets ($111.7 million in New York, $53.3 million in Europe, and $63.5 million in Mexico) (*El Porvenir*, November 20, 1991).

SUPPLIER NETWORKS

As was noted at the outset of this chapter, the new forms of organizing production have given rise to a series of changes in interfirm relationships. Companies require more expeditious methods for transferring inputs and products between suppliers and customers. The conditions demanded by quality programs and just-in-time production[31] lead to closer links between firms and stimulate the appearance of supplier networks. These take shape through a process in which customers and suppliers work closely together to achieve several objectives: First, to guarantee the quality of required inputs, not only through traditional quality controls and overall specifications, but also through an exchange of information on the respective processes and through mutual feedback on problems which arise in their use or manufacture. Second, to guarantee JIT by reducing the time for scheduling orders and deliveries, thus reducing inventories and being able to offer customers greater flexibility and the incorporation of last-minute modifications. Third, to strengthen the bonds between suppliers and customers such that together they form a bloc against growing foreign competition. (If a customer is used to working with a supplier who makes special accommodations under extraordinary circumstances, that customer will not lightly switch to a new supplier unless the latter promises to be equally accommodating.)

Transnational firms were the first to introduce this new type of relationship in Mexico. Their presence in Mexico, especially in the automotive industry, dates back decades. However, when they located in Mexico they first took on the same characteristics as Mexican firms. The advantages they enjoyed from a closed and protected economy meant that they functioned with a certain degree of inefficiency and underproductivity similar to what prevailed in Mexican domestic industry. They also enjoyed the same high profit margin that results from scant competition and strong market control. Thus, when faced with economic opening, they too had to modify their relationship with international markets. However, their natural links with parent firms abroad facilitated the change enormously.

It is in this sense that transnational firms play a very important role as catalysts in the modernization process. These firms were the first in Mexico to promote standardizing quality by working with their suppliers. Ford, for example, demands that its suppliers furnish proof of statistical controls in the production of parts.

---

[31] Just-in-time delivery not only reduces the costs of maintaining large inventories; it also reduces waste and forces the correction of errors in product quality.

Further, Ford has made sure that its suppliers have the capacity to fill orders with quality parts within the appropriate time frame.

In its pursuit of such guarantees, Ford signed an economic cooperation agreement with the Quality Center at the Monterrey Technological Institute. At Ford's request, this institution developed a statistical process control program which allows engineers and workers to anticipate defects and monitor quality in parts production. Ford now requires its suppliers to have a certificate of training from that institution. The program has been adopted by a wide range of industries. Over the last ten years, the Monterrey Technological Institute has provided training in statistical process control to employees from more than six hundred firms from all areas of Mexico.[32]

Another example is Burroughs Welcome de México, a pharmaceutical industry with British capital. Since 1988 the company has had a program in place to develop suppliers in which it asks them to meet a series of specifications and then evaluates their performance quarterly. The firm gets to know its suppliers' plants, equipment, and processes, and even takes suppliers to visit other plants in Mexico and abroad where the requested standards are met so that they may observe and learn how to meet them.

Although most of the Mexican supplier firms I visited were not subject to thorough quality audits, many supply transnational firms which, as we have seen, have advanced mechanisms to evaluate suppliers' quality. Thus, these firms have not only improved the quality of their products, they have also learned how to evaluate their own suppliers. It is possible to foresee a near future when linkages will extend to many other companies not directly related to the transnational firms.

As mentioned earlier, aside from allowing quality control over inputs, the new relationships with suppliers give firms much more flexibility, permitting them to respond more quickly to the unexpected changes in demand that characterize current market behavior. In this sense, greater proximity to suppliers is an additional advantage for producers.

To illustrate how this type of relationship has developed in the corporations studied, consider the case of a Monterrey automotive parts producer. We shall call this firm *F*; its customers are the large auto assembly plants located in northern and central Mexico,

---

[32]In Monterrey, employees of Vidriera Monterrey, Ford Motor Company, Industrias Monterrey, Conek, Camisa, Polienvases, Grupo Industrial Benavides, Asfaltos Polímeros, Lámparas General Electric, Vitroplast, Multilec, Tubacero, Vitroflex, Vitrocrisa, Telmex, Lamosa, Metalsa Nemak, Pyosa, Productos Químicos Allen, Quimobásicos, and many other firms have attended these courses.

which we shall call C. Since its main input is steel, the firm has a large Mexican steel supplier, *DS*, and several foreign suppliers, *FS*.

F has sought closer links with both Mexican (*DS*) and foreign (*FS*) suppliers to achieve a JIT system. The main difference between the two types of suppliers is product quality. However, this difference has lessened in recent years. *F* has never had quality problems with *FS*, having achieved transaction levels with zero rejects. With *DS*, rejects have been reduced from 3.6 percent three years ago to less than 1 percent today. This has been achieved through a new relationship between *F* and *DS* in which they meet weekly in *F*'s plant with representatives of supply, production control, and quality control departments from each firm. Quality problems and problems with scheduling orders are discussed at these meetings, and a feedback process takes place as *DS*'s representatives can observe the production process and the parts that are manufactured with the inputs supplied by their firms.

One of the important advances achieved by *F* in its relationship with *DS* is just-in-time deliveries. Three years ago *F*'s supply system consisted of large purchases to cover needs over several months. Today inventory time has been reduced to one week. In other words, in this relationship *F* reviews its orders on a weekly basis. At the same time, the volume of input orders is calculated according to purchase orders from *F*'s customers, who are assigned a given week each month to submit their orders. These automotive parts orders are translated into kilograms or tons of steel, establishing the amount of raw material that *F* will ask *DS* to provide.

Delivery time is four weeks. During week 1, *F* looks at what it will use in week 5. The agreement with *DS* is that it must produce the part in week 3 and deliver it in week 4. Previously, an entire month's orders were lumped together for deliveries the following month, but often the steel that arrived first was not needed until the end of the month and went into inventory, while urgent orders were often delayed.

F notes that since they began this system two years ago they have never failed a customer; rather, it is the latter who frequently ask for last-minute changes or adjustments.[33] If *DS* has not started production on the order, it will accept modifications. If production has begun, *F* must reprogram this surplus product for another customer in order to keep zero inventory. *F*'s ability to respond immediately to its customers and *DS*'s ability to respond imme-

---

[33]To prevent unforeseen problems, *F* has signed an agreement with *DS* which covers all of these possibilities. According to *F*, "If we happen to receive steel that does not work for us, the supplier has to produce a special batch to meet specifications in less than ten days. This has happened only three times in a two-year period."

diately to *F* are highly appreciated by the customer and strengthen supplier networks. Clearly the domestic supplier's physical proximity makes this kind of cooperation easier. However, given Mexico's uneven economic development, it is not always possible to find suppliers who can meet JIT requirements. For example, another firm studied had a very difficult time avoiding accumulating large inventories because it could not find dependable, well-organized suppliers for certain products such as wood, a sector where suppliers with these characteristics are practically nonexistent.

The advantages of having suppliers close by are clearer if we look at *F*'s situation with regard to its foreign suppliers. *F* buys its products from *FS* because the type of steel these suppliers produce is not made in Mexico. However, the delivery time from foreign suppliers is quadruple that of domestic suppliers. In fact, the time frame goes from weekly to monthly, although the control mechanisms are exactly the same so that inventories of more than a month of this type of steel are eliminated. Therefore, *F* considers that its relationship with *FS* is also JIT.

In the case of suppliers located in the United States, delivery time is four months (five months for suppliers in Germany and Japan): as a general rule, steel manufacture takes ninety days, plus three weeks for rail transport and one week for border crossing. Mexican firms expect that an order placed in month 1 will be to them in month 5, and suppliers are instructed how to distribute each order among various plants. Some problems arise in transport because smaller orders leave railcar space unutilized and trains wait to fill this free space; also, trains are often delayed en route or at border crossings. Both of these factors are beyond the control of either the customer or the supplier. (For all but German suppliers, price is for goods delivered at the border.) A significant disadvantage to using foreign suppliers is that *F*'s customers lose the option to make last-minute changes in their orders. As one informant observed:

> Once the steel is at sea nothing can be done, so the person in charge of production is in close contact with the customers to get them to be as precise as possible in their orders. Producers know beforehand how difficult it is to make changes in a part made of imported steel, so they pay closer attention and do not make changes. But when they know that a part is domestic steel, they wait until the last minute, anticipating changes.

Thus, flexibility in inputs depends on supplier proximity as well as on the type of relationship that exists between customer and supplier and the latter's willingness to accept its customer's last-minute modifications. Theoretically, then, if Mexican firms develop adequate quality standards and delivery times, they will be preferred over foreign suppliers. Hence the importance of network diversification and supplier development programs.

Supplier development programs sometimes include mid-sized service-providing firms. The case of Burroughs Welcome is one example. When this firm began conducting part of its manufacturing processes in sterile rooms, it developed a series of specifications on construction and installations which forced providers of these services to change their procedures and quality standards. Despite the fact that the Mexican Ministry of Health has similar specifications, the service providers had to repeat their procedures several times before they met the standard that Burroughs Welcome demanded. Thus, quality requirements not only drive modifications in one given branch of industry, they may also spread to service providers and suppliers from a broader range of industries.

This means that customers' needs and requirements are part of what drives technological modernization. Put another way, the firm's degree of modernization is related to product characteristics and to the market at which it is aimed. Clearly plants that supply transnational firms are further along in their restructuring process. For example, Imsa, a supplier of galvanized sheet metal, must meet specifications set by Whirlpool, Carrier, and the automotive industry; Metalsa gets specifications from Chrysler, General Motors, Ford, and Nissan.

Meanwhile, and despite the fact that most domestic firms studied do not yet conduct quality audits with their suppliers, the most developed firms have begun to demand international quality standards. Thus we find that Nemak, an Alfa subsidiary, has a program to develop Mexican suppliers which has enabled it to decrease its imports of inputs. As recently as 1990, Nemak imported 80 percent of its raw materials; in 1992 it imported only 40 percent.

The complementarity that large Monterrey firms seek when they form partnerships or acquire new firms fosters the consolidation of domestic supplier networks with whom negotiations over specifications and last-minute adjustments become much easier. When Alfa entered into partnership with Metecno of Italy to form Galvamet for the production of galvanized and painted steel sheet panels, it located its new plant in San Nicolás, Nuevo León, near Galvak and Polioles. These two firms belonging to the Alfa group became Galvamet's suppliers of galvanized steel sheet and poly-urethane, respectively. Cydsa acquired San Marcos (located in the state of Aguascalientes), a firm that produces blankets, towels, and quilts. San Marcos became a part of Cydsa's fibers division along with Crysel, Dasa, and Rayón. In this way, Cydsa has become vertically integrated within its textile branch, producing every-thing from raw material to finished product and having assured suppliers.

Vertical integration is not new. In fact, it is how the Monterrey Group was built throughout the twentieth century. But it takes on another dimension with supplier development programs. This is not the old vertical integration, which sought to monopolize the market by controlling prices and all phases of production. Now it is a matter of achieving the greatest possible degree of dependability by building a solid network of suppliers. As noted earlier, domestic suppliers can be audited much more easily and can adapt more quickly to product modifications. Further, the development of domestic suppliers has a financial advantage: the corporation's unified accounting system allows it to count sales among subsid-iaries as consolidated sales, which indeed they are, so that the firm also gains a captive customer who contributes to the firm's balance sheet, an important factor in the value of company stock and also a tax savings.

The requisites for successful consolidation of this type are process complementarity and administrative autonomy among production units. In effect, the firms of the Monterrey Group have returned to vertical integration after jettisoning the model of extensive diversification which they followed during the 1970s, with dire results in the 1980s.

An additional effect of supplier development programs relates to technology. The customer's quality requirements and specifica-tions for the manufacture of new products force suppliers to introduce technological improvements and innovations in their products, giving rise to technological modernization. Frequently the source of this modernization is the foreign partner in a technol-ogy alliance.

TECHNOLOGY ALLIANCES

Our research into the role that technology investment plays in restructuring produced an extremely uneven picture. On the one hand we found firms that have invested a major part of their resources in technological modernization through technology alli-ances with foreign firms, technology transfers through the pur-chase or acquisition of equipment and systems, and the development of proprietary technology in research and development departments. On the other hand, we found that most firms do not have a complete technological modernization program and lack R&D departments.

In the case of the latter group, our interviews uncovered persisting traditional concepts regarding technology: decisions on the choice and acquisition of technology frequently depend on the individual experience of the director or head of a given department and that person's ability to choose and assimilate technology developed in other countries, as well as on the ability of the firm's engineers to adapt and improve it. In many cases engineers had introduced real innovations as they modified old machines to meet customers' new specifications, but these innovations were often weakened or introduced with inadequate preplanning.

When a firm lacks a clear technology policy, selecting a technology depends on whether it will allow the firm to meet its customers' specifications. Profitability criteria are also important when acquiring technology, since investing in high-precision technology may be hard to justify if the new technology does not produce a payoff in the market. Another criterion in choosing a technology is its adaptability, since certain technologies may be designed for volumes larger than the purchaser produces, or they may call for a raw material that is hard to obtain. Some firms buy technology that they have been able to test and evaluate in their own plants. Still others make their selection after looking for the best products and then buying the technology that produces them, though this strategy does not always produce optimum results since the same machinery can yield less in Mexico than in its place of origin because of infrastructure problems and the lack of qualified personnel. This results in the underutilization of the technology and a concomitant resource drain.

Technology may be acquired in a package that includes installation and training in its use, or the purchasers may implement it through a process of "reverse engineering." The latter consists of taking equipment apart, understanding how it works, and putting it back together once the technology has been understood (CIDE 1989). One of Cydsa's Fibras Químicas plants bought a technology package from the Netherlands; when the technology suppliers had to postpone installation and training, Monterrey engineers started up the machinery on their own and put the technology to work.

In general, it appears that the process of deciding what technology to acquire generally starts when and where there is a problem that needs to be solved. In this sense, department heads must sell their superiors on the long-term value of the technology investment.

Taking into account the fact that advanced technology and automation do not eliminate a firm's operational problems but only displace them to new areas (Schoenberger 1989a), if departments do not make technology decisions jointly the result will merely be a transfer of problems from one department to another. For example, adopting a new technology in one department generates the need for a new kind of worker, a series of indirect costs, material costs, and problems in the utilization of installed capacity, with repercussions throughout the rest of the organization.

Although businessmen are apparently not encountering legal or bureaucratic restrictions on technology imports, they are finding infrastructure deficiencies within their own firms (such as a lack of qualified personnel to operate it) and deficiencies in Mexico's infrastructure (transportation, energy, public services, etc.). The former indicate the firms' lack of comprehensive planning, while the latter indicate the same for the country and the region.

In some cases the deficiencies extend to a lack of appropriate service providers, when the implementation of new product or process technology requires special installations or services (a special electrical supply, water or vapor systems, special insulation, etc.). In these cases the engineers must again apply their creativity to adapt the technology to prevailing conditions.

It would appear that few firms understand the new role that industrial research and development is playing worldwide. As recently as the 1960s and 1970s, a new product was guaranteed to remain profitable for seven to ten years. However, the life cycle of new products has dropped to about two or three years.[34] This directly affects the activity of R&D departments, since the move from idea to project must now be much quicker. Moreover, technology must be viewed as an integral process within the firm, and it must be closely linked to the business, giving technological innovation a key role it did not have before (Armstrong 1991). In other words, technological innovation must take place in R&D departments, but it must also respond to the needs of other departments such as engineering, manufacturing, sales, finance, services, etc.

One firm in the Monterrey Group that stresses the need to integrate technology is Vitro Envases. This division of the Vitro group instituted a technology development department to link technology decisions with marketing strategies and customer satisfaction. The department develops technologies to resolve problems or bottlenecks and to improve the production process overall. The department's communication with Vitro Envases's

---

[34]Televised conference with W.J. Spencer, of IBM's Research and Development Department, 1991.

various plants is a two-way process: the technology development department proposes ways to optimize production, while the plants report problems and ask the technology department to identify what equipment is needed to correct them. If the equipment does not exist on the market, they develop it; if it does exist, they select the most appropriate application. The department installs the equipment and, in conjunction with the company's education and training department, transmits the know-how.

It is no coincidence that technology development plays a fundamental role at Vitro, a company which has moved very successfully into the world of global production. In fact, this new view of technology as linked to the production process is precisely what has changed the criteria for plant location within the process of globalization. Under previous forms of the international division of labor, R&D tended to locate in core countries, component production took place in another area, and final product assembly was done in low-wage countries. Globalization has produced strategies which are increasingly oriented toward a spatial division of labor based on more or less integrated product lines in various regions of the world, which means that all of these phases are carried out simultaneously for each product in each location (Schoenberger 1989a).

In practice, a large part of scientific research and technological innovation continues to be done in the developed countries. To resolve this apparent contradiction, we must distinguish between two types of technological research: *basic* research requiring complex installations and pursuing scientific knowledge not closely linked to the daily problems of production, and *operational* research aimed at solving difficulties in the manufacturing process and improving product quality. It is operational research that is being decentralized to subsidiaries within and outside the country of origin, while basic research remains in home offices.[35]

In this context, Vitro-Whirlpool's Acros industrial center offers an interesting example; production is organized by product line and supported by an R&D department. This industrial center near Monterrey (constructed at a cost of $150 million) has the installed capacity to produce 500,000 refrigerators and 300,000 washing machines per year.[36] Its goal is vertical integration of the entire

---

[35]The German firm Siemens carries out all of its research and development activities at the operational level within its subsidiaries, while basic research is centralized in Germany. But scientists in the central laboratory must be able to sell some of their basic research to plant directors of operations (*Fortune*, April 20, 1992).

[36]It is expected that this plant will increase the household appliances division's sales to nearly $400 million and that exports will rise from their current level of 5 or 6 percent to 35 percent of total production.

production process for domestic appliances in its six manufacturing plants, which produce all the main components, from compressors to final product assembly (*El Norte*, September 1, 1992). The close proximity of the technology center to the production plants will allow for direct, ongoing contact during different stages of the production process, enhancing integration between technology development and production. The experience of this plant contributes an important element to the discussion on whether R&D departments will be moved to Third World countries (Schoenberger 1989a, 1989b; Gertler 1988). It appears likely that operational research will move outside the country of origin in order to integrate with local plants engaged in manufacturing.

On the other hand, the features of Vitro's partnership with Whirlpool brings us to another element which plays an important role in technology transfer: technology alliances. These alliances have become the most effective way for Monterrey plants to incorporate technological innovations. There are many types of partnerships, ranging from joint plant ownership to simple agreements for the exchange of technological information. The Vitro-Whirlpool partnership and the resulting formation of the Vitromatic company is an example of the first type. Vitro has entered into a number of other technology alliances, foremost among them its 1991 alliance with World Tableware International, a leading U.S. flatware manufacturer. Under their agreement, Vitro acquired 49 percent of the Amsilco Division, with plants in the United States, while World Tableware obtained the same number of shares in Vitro's Vitrocrisa division, with plants in various parts of Mexico (*El Norte*, March 25, 1992; see appendix 1). The agreement provides a wealth of technological information to each partner.

Meanwhile, Vitro's partnership with Corning, producer of glassware for homes, laboratories, and communications applications, has turned out to be an excellent means for Vitro to acquire new technology. (Corning, a leader in the field, introduced the concept of cooking in glass after it developed highly heat-resistant borosilicate glass; Corning has thirty-three testing laboratories.) The agreement with Corning includes the exchange of technology, research, and engineering resources for product development (*El Porvenir*, March 26, 1992).

Another example is Nemak, the Alfa subsidiary in Nuevo León, which manufactures aluminum cylinder heads and was created through a coinvestment with Ford. In 1989 a new partner joined Nemak; the Italian firm Teksid (a Fiat subsidiary) acquired 20 percent of Nemak's capital, bringing with it an important new technology, the semipermanent gravity mold process (*El Norte*,

January 30, 1992).[37] Ford retains 20 percent, and Alfa controls the firm with the remaining 60 percent.

It is important to emphasize that within the NAFTA framework these partnerships must evolve toward market complementarity, that is, agreements to produce different products, such as agreements in place between automotive firms in Canada and the United States by which each firm concentrates on producing a certain model of automobile, complementing the other's market and sharing distribution channels.

Foreign firms in Mexico used to receive all technology from their parent firms,[38] and therefore had no research and development departments. This situation was largely due to the lack of trademark protection in Mexico, particularly in the chemical and pharmaceutical industries. But with the 1991 passage of the Law to Promote and Protect Intellectual Property this problem has been largely resolved. This new legislation places strict controls on the issuance of trademarks and patents, which can be given only by the Ministry of Commerce and Industrial Development. The law also extends protection to ideas by permitting the registration of utility models and industrial secrets and designs. According to the law, a utility model includes any modifications to an apparatus or tool that improves its operation. This aspect of the law protects innovations that arise in workshops and small and mid-sized firms. Patents remain in effect for twenty years; they are issued for inventions in pharmaceuticals and general medicine, as well as for products based on biotechnological or chemical innovations.[39] Registration of advertising slogans, trademarks, and industrial designs remains in effect for fifteen years. The Mexican Institute for Intellectual Property was created to oversee implementation of the new law.

To summarize, integrating technology into the production process requires a comprehensive understanding of the new requirements of industry and of the international market. The global market calls for linking R&D with marketing, sharing visions and

---

[37]Similar partnerships have been established by other firms not part of the Monterrey Group, such as the Pyosa chemical firm, which arranged a coinvestment with Bitossi (an Italian company) for the creation of Esmacer, a new company in the Monterrey area. In this case Pyosa holds 49 percent of the shares, and Bitossi, which brought its leading-edge technology for manufacturing ceramic products, has control of the new company. Likewise, Metalsa, a subsidiary of the Proeza group, has a partnership with A.O. Smith; the latter gives Metalsa access to all of its technological information in exchange for royalty payments.

[38]Author interviews with representatives of Conek, a subsidiary of Caterpillar in the United States, and Burroughs Welcome de México, a subsidiary of the Welcome Foundation in Great Britain (August 1990).

[39]The law also provides patents for varieties of vegetables, microorganisms with productive or medicinal uses, metal and other alloys, and food and beverages.

objectives, designing plans and programs, and establishing a division of labor to achieve the final product—in other words, working together (Armstrong 1991).

This new concept is beginning to spread among the Monterrey firms, but only a few have the experience required to put it into practice. For years only Vitro and Alfa made sustained efforts to innovate. Vitro began benchmarking in technology little more than twenty years ago, when it created a research and development laboratory called Vitrotec.[40] It tracked technological advances in firms worldwide that employed technologies of interest to Vitro. However, Vitro had trouble matching these technologies to the operational needs of its plants. Vitro later carried out research efforts at its FAMA (Fabricantes de Máquinas) machine manufacturing plant, where technology allowed Vitro to change molds rapidly so that it could produce either very large or very small batches depending on the market niches for its crystal. This flexibility is a great advantage under the new models of production. In fact, this ability to produce for small market niches was one of the contributions Vitro brought when it purchased Anchor Glass. In exchange Anchor taught Vitro how to achieve a greater economy in personnel and greater labor productivity in the United States (*América Economía*, March 1992). Corning, Vitro's new partner, has also shown an interest in this flexibility, which it applies in the market for cut crystal produced by Vitro and sold by Corning under the Kristaluxus brand name.

On the other hand, through Hylsa, its most important subsidiary, Alfa has been a technology exporter for more than thirty years, ever since its researchers developed the technique to produce sponge iron. Hylsa currently has a training program in using that technology, in which close to 350 foreign technicians (primarily from the Middle East) are enrolled. The training program alone provides the firm with an income of close to $6 million. Hylsa's technology division has plans to sell sponge iron plants to Algeria, Syria, Turkey, and Thailand; plants are already in operation in Indonesia, Iran, India, and Malaysia.

Hylsa recently developed a leading-edge technology in direct reduction, in which steel is produced from sheet in reactors, eliminating the need for blast furnaces. Hylsa has sold the technology to India and will install it there, and it will sell technology and support to a plant starting up in Venezuela, another in Brazil, three in Iran, four in Iraq, and four in Indonesia.

---

[40]Benchmarking is a search for the best work practices in a certain area, such as production, customer service, technology, etc.

Other Monterrey Group firms besides Vitro and Alfa have recently taken important steps in technology development. Imsa, for example, through its Multypanel subsidiary, has developed proprietary technology which brought it into the global market for commercial refrigeration equipment. It operates in partnership with the U.S. firm Melt-Span, with investments in Poland and other Eastern European countries. In addition to foreign competition, Multypanel is also competing with Alfa's Galvamet plant and its new technology for double-faced galvanized and painted sheet metal.

Cydsa has invested $12 million in its Bonlam plant in San Luis Potosí, which produces nonwoven fabrics from polypropylene (Agribon) for disposable diapers, medical apparel, and other clothing. It has also carried out experiments and demonstrations for close to two hundred agriculturalists on the usefulness of Agribon as greenhouse material. In the experiments, the use of Agribon increased productivity from 8 to 60 tons per hectare. This technology forms part of Cydsa's program to create new markets for its technological developments (*El Norte*, March 12, 1991).

Finally, in 1991 Visa invested $260 million in modernization, expansion, and technology. Its Fábricas Monterrey (Famosa) subsidiary, with plants in Monterrey, Toluca, Orizaba, and Ensenada, produces packaging materials. It has built a line to manufacture nondetachable pop-top lids for aluminum cans (with a $38 million investment) using leading-edge technology supported by its U.S. partner, Ball Metal Group. This new product will make Famosa more independent of Ball Metal, which formerly supplied it with the can tops. Visa also invested $68 million in 1992 in leading-edge technology to manufacture bottle caps in lots small enough to satisfy clients' specialized needs.

Economic globalization has unleashed a series of important processes in Mexican industry, in which we can discern mechanisms for transmitting and stimulating technological investment. These include programs to develop suppliers, networks for technology transfer through partnerships and coinvestments with foreign firms, and independent technology development. The firms that support integrating technology into the production process have accomplished this goal through the total quality concept, which is part of the new production systems and which includes a transformation of labor relations inside the plants. Quality programs and a new relationship with labor are essential for implementing flexible production, as we shall see in the next chapter.

5

Total Quality Programs and the New Labor Relations Model

The transformations that have taken place in firms' relations with international markets have their counterpart in the changes required inside plants in order to introduce new forms of organization and flexible production. Flexible production grew out of the crisis in work organization as developed in Taylorism and Fordism; the rigidity of the old pattern—designed for the mass production of standardized products—is incompatible with the characteristics of an increasingly diversified and competitive market.

Economic growth is seen less and less as depending on rigid resources (e.g., large, specialized machinery, serial production, assembly lines, and workers performing a single task), and more and more on flexible ones. The need to reduce costs, eliminate waste, and optimize competitiveness has led firms to pursue inventory reduction, total quality control, work teams in which workers and bosses participate in decision making, and, above all, a multiskilled worker capable of performing various tasks. Flexible production alters the traditional conditions of work, including wages, length of the workday, skill structure, and job stability (Boyer 1988, 1990; Leborgne and Lipietz 1988; Piore 1990).

This new scheme is only now beginning to gain ground in Mexico. Countries like Mexico, which were never fully integrated into economic development, configured different systems characterized by external dependency and internal protectionism. The crisis and the sudden economic opening promoted by the federal government left Mexico exposed to the patterns of work organization introduced by transnational firms. This process is moving so rapidly that at times Mexico does not seem to be sufficiently prepared.

However, in the case of Monterrey Group firms, the existence of a particular form of company trade unionism ("white" unions) has facilitated the unilateral adoption of flexible production without the participation of unions. This has been accomplished through quality programs, which modify the process of technological innovation and also the administrative structure of the firms, with important consequences for labor relations as a whole.

QUALITY PROGRAMS

Most of the firms studied have adopted some type of quality program.[41] However, because they are subsidiaries of large corporations, their implementation of quality programs takes place against the backdrop of a broader modification in the corporation-subsidiary relationship. As we saw in chapter 3, the corporations under study modified the structure of their firms at the start of the 1980s, abandoning the model of diversification and centralized management that they had followed in the 1970s. Currently, the original groups are unfolding into a multitude of firms with a greater degree of autonomy; besides increasing their productivity, this enables them to increase channels for capitalization and partnerships with U.S. firms. For example, Visa divided in two, giving rise to Femsa, which controls stockholders' shares in the brewing, mineral water, soft drinks, and packing industries. Femsa in turn divided into two independent companies, one financial and the other industrial; Visa owns 60 percent of each. Twenty percent of Femsa's capital is owned by the International Finance Corporation, and 20 percent circulates on the domestic and foreign stock markets (*El Norte*, November 29 and December 6, 1991). Each of these firms is managed independently and has its own board of directors, but they are still controlled by the founding family through stock ownership.

Corporations do not reorganize for financial reasons alone. Reorganization also achieves a real decentralization of functions. Although corporation heads still monitor each firm's performance (financial statements, market share, product development, and production and quality achievements) the decision-making process has been reversed: subsidiaries now present proposals to the corporation on possible partnerships, coinvestments, market expansion, or market integration. In this sense, one of the corporation's most important functions is financial: it must work to opti-

---

[41]In order to analyze the changes within the firms, we used information obtained in direct interviews with officers and managers, on one hand, and with workers and union leaders on the other. This was done at a total of nine plants (see appendix 2). We also visited the workplace to observe work processes directly.

mize the group's resources so that it can back its subsidiaries with large investment funds. In daily practice, the corporation tends to be limited to providing some services in computer systems, legal affairs, financial matters, and human resources, always at the request of the subsidiary, while the subsidiaries are becoming increasingly independent in their management.

This reorganization at the group level is reflected within the plants in their move to quality programs. Twenty years ago, quality meant satisfying specifications provided by a laboratory or a quality control department. Today it means meeting customers' needs. The new definition goes beyond the relationship between quality and product, to extend to service. The product is redefined to include intangibles such as delivery time, warranties, etc.

However, although all the firms under study have adopted some type of quality program, in few cases did these firms take into account the implications for the production process, plant design and distribution, work tempo, production run size, and quality control mechanisms. Rather, the implementation of these programs reveals some inconsistencies: administrative structures are being streamlined in all the plants, but we found very few cases where plant design eliminated the distance between planning, engineering, management, and the factory floor. This is due in part to the high costs of remodeling plant structure. Therefore, as long as department proximity is not viewed as absolutely necessary to guarantee competitiveness, the status quo will probably persist. Among companies where we found plans to modify firm layout is Metalsa, a firm in the Proeza group. In order to prepare for foreign competition, Metalsa developed a strategy that includes adapting processes and investments to concentrate plants and relocate presses for maximum efficiency.

Monterrey firms seem to be enthusiastically adopting the new management techniques coming from Japan, Europe, and the United States. However, as is the case with quality programs, assimilation of the new models is not achieved automatically, since it presupposes an overall understanding of what the change means, as well as the ability to put it into practice. While all firms understand the need to adopt a philosophy of quality, the way in which they have appropriated this philosophy has consisted basically of providing training to department heads through frequently unsystematic courses and seminars. The same firm may select one component each from the Deming, Juran, Crosby,

Ishikawa, and Taguchi models.[42] Adopting such a medley of components can actually hamper rather than simplify a firm's functioning. Thus, the main obstacles to the adoption of new management approaches, outlined in response to our questionnaires, were: "the confusion between traditional forms of management and flexible techniques" and "a resistance to change, above all at the management level."

The ease or difficulty with which the new approaches are adopted is strongly influenced by the age and size of the plant. The older the plant, the harder it is to change, since its physical layout and organizational structure correspond to traditional production methods, radically opposed to what is now viewed as modernization. In comparing two related plants in Monterrey and Apodaca, Nuevo León, respectively, we were able to see the difficulties for plants that have strong traditional roots. The Apodaca plant is much newer and has fewer employees than the Monterrey plant. Flexible forms of organizing production were adopted in their entirety in the Apodaca plant, while the 35-year-old Monterrey plant's efforts to modernize were hindered by the design of the plant and resistance to change, primarily from middle management. Similarly, Vitro's new Acros complex confirms that it is easier to innovate when plants are planned with new production concepts in mind from the outset.

Regarding modifications in quality control mechanisms, the firms seem to find themselves in transition. At this stage, they are concentrating on training workers in techniques for statistical process control to monitor quality. Inventory reduction and JIT were found in most firms. Work teams and quality circles (implemented under a wide variety of names and operating in different ways) also seem to be in vogue. It was not possible to determine how important they are for the production process; measuring their impact would require further research.

According to a business consultant I interviewed, most firms confuse flexible management methods with the adoption of isolated quality circles. One large firm that adopted this form of team work found itself with a major management problem; the quality circles began to develop an informal structure which paralleled the institutional structure, generating confusion and high administrative costs. This seems to indicate that when limited modifications are introduced but the traditional framework is left intact, workers

---

[42]The Deming, Crosby, and Juran models are essentially oriented toward quality achieved through the manufacturing process. For Deming, it is achieved by means of statistical process control; for Juran, by means of the vertical chain of operations that begins with design; and for Crosby by a change in organizational culture. The Japanese models integrate quality with service and customer needs.

receive ambiguous signals and this creates confusion in the organization.

The adoption of advanced technology, the integration of new flexible management techniques to achieve total quality, and a clear move toward developing multiskilled workers are all taking place within the Monterrey firms in a context of extremely rigid structures which are resistant to change.[43]

Once again it is the large corporations that have led the way in developing total quality programs. Crysel, a Cydsa subsidiary in Guadalajara which produces acrylic fiber, won the National Quality Prize in 1991 by significantly reducing its consumption of raw materials, directly marketing its products, and increasing sales by 8 percent. This plant is the most important acrylic fiber producer in Latin America and ranks seventh worldwide. Its quality program, which consists of an ongoing search for innovative work methods, is based on three principles: create value for the customer, develop human resources on the job, and work toward becoming internationally competitive. The program involves constant personnel training, team work, multiskilling, flexible production, computerized process control, innovative station design, and attainment of workers' individual goals. Under this program, production per worker went from 40 tons per year in 1985 to 72 tons per year in 1991, increasing the plant's annual production from 55,000 to 78,000 tons. Reworking was reduced by 98 percent, water usage dropped 55 percent, and waste fell to between 2 and 2.5 percent (author interview).

The 1991 Nuevo León Quality Prize, with standards similar to those of the National Prize, also went to a plant belonging to the Cydsa group: Master Pack-Propirey. Its quality program has been defined by its director as a socio-technical system. This program enabled the firm to reduce returns by 50 percent in just one year. The main feature of this system is the elimination of supervisors on the production line and their replacement by direct worker control.

One problem produced by this system is a high turnover rate, since workers are constantly in training and advancing to other jobs or resigning to take better jobs in other firms. Seven percent of total man-hours at work are devoted to training. The design and implementation of the program was based on customer ratings, interviews with users, and a cost-benefit analysis which included

---

[43]In fact, of the 7,000 firms registered with the Chamber of Manufacturers (CAINTRA), only 500 firms (less than 2 percent) formally and systematically apply total quality programs. This contrasts with the 60 to 70 percent participation in these programs on the part of firms in advanced countries (*El Porvenir*, June 12, 1992).

the total cost for improving quality versus total sales by specific market.

Among the incentives for implementing quality programs are the awards granted by the Mexican government, international customers, or the corporations themselves to their most efficient subsidiaries. Metalsa has won a number of awards: five Pentastars from Chrysler, a Q-1 certificate from Ford, six awards from General Motors, and Nissan's Yushu Shoh. The Vitro group has an internal prize which it awards to its best plants. In 1992, the winning firm was Vitro-Flex, which devoted between 4 and 5 percent of its man-hours to employee training. This firm produces a million automobile windows annually for Chrysler, Ford, and Nissan; 25 percent of its production is exported, mainly to South America, Europe, and China. Its quality model, which began by defining the characteristics of the product Vitro-Flex wanted to supply to its customers, is based on statistical process control.[44] The elements of the model are customer satisfaction, leadership, worker involvement, information analysis, planning, quality assurance, and evaluation of results.

However, the optimism that managers expressed regarding the implementation of quality programs contrasts somewhat with the views of workers, who seem to perceive the innovations as increasing their responsibility and work load without sufficient rewards, as we shall see in the following section.

LABOR RELATIONS

To simplify the analysis of the findings at the level of the workers, we divided the plants into three groups according to the level of flexible production observed by the researchers (see appendix 2). The first group is made up of the firms that seem to have fully adopted flexible production techniques; that is, plants that have been designed around flexibility, from the layout of the plant to the planning of production. The second group includes firms that have adopted some elements of the new production techniques, and the third group includes plants that essentially operate under the traditional forms of Taylorism and Fordism.

Besides the sources of information mentioned earlier, the analysis is based on the results of in-depth interviews conducted with thirty workers outside of the plants. Interviews lasted two hours on average, and the information gathered allowed us to

---

[44]A quality control system implemented by the workers themselves which consists of maintaining a statistical record of the characteristics of the parts they manufacture.

pinpoint the most problematic aspects of modernization for labor relations within the plants.

For the analysis of the firms in the first group, which we call Group A, we specified an extreme case in which flexible management is already fully operational. In none of the Monterrey firms to which we had access did we find such a situation; therefore, we selected a subsidiary of a firm outside of the Monterrey Group, whose characteristics provide a point of reference for understanding the changes in labor relations.[45]

The selected plant, Plant A, makes heavy machinery for its parent company in the United States, operates with 100 percent U.S. capital, and has 18 departments with 750 workers. At Plant A the modernization process is being carried out at both the technical and management levels. In 1988 the plant's layout was modified for flexible production techniques. Most machines are programmable and, despite their large size, are arranged in cells, so that a single worker can operate one of three different machines consecutively or even simultaneously. This introduces a great deal of flexibility; it becomes possible to manufacture different products according to demand and the changing requirements of JIT production; and set-up time for changing machines from one type of product to another is reduced. Specifications arrive from the United States via fax or computer, are distributed to each department, and then go to the workers through the Kanbam system. Inventories have been practically eliminated, since trucks loaded with just-finished products leave the plant several times a day en route to the United States. Clearly the characteristics of the production process at Plant A require multiskilled workers, which is why 100 percent of the plant's workers are trained to perform various tasks.

The plant switched to this system in 1988. The change included reducing the labor force from 2,000 to 750 workers; helpers were laid off and only specialized workers were retained. The firm's employees have been assembled in "continuous improvement groups," made up of workers, supervisors, and engineers who meet to solve problems and propose improvements in the production process. Before they can move into higher job categories, workers are trained for three months; they are promoted based on the results of an evaluation. Workers also attend classes in total quality production. The tendency is to leave quality control in the hands of the workers: previously there were two quality

---

[45]Before 1983, this firm was in partnership with a Monterrey Group firm from which it inherited the union; therefore relations between the firm and the union are very similar to those that prevail within the Monterrey Group, facilitating our using it as a model.

supervisors per department; now there is only one or, in some departments, none.

Apparently production has been structurally transformed in Plant A, according to the indicators we used to measure the adoption of flexible production techniques (reduction of job positions and categories, quality monitoring by workers, use of JIT, task rotation, work teams, and programmable machines). This has enabled the firm to noticeably improve its market position.

Although they have not reached the same levels in adopting flexible techniques, several plants belonging to the Monterrey Group come very close to this model, especially some producers of glass, chemical fibers and products, automotive parts, and plastics. However, neither from interviews with workers from these plants nor from direct observation were we able to find any real worker participation in decision making or worker control over production or assembly lines. For example, workers cannot stop the production line when they find a mistake, as happens in Japanese plants. Supervisors continue to concentrate authority and control over the process. In fact, quite a few workers interviewed complained about their supervisors because the latter do not seem to welcome the workers' suggestions when they meet in quality circles.

The second group, Group B, is exemplified by a Mexican-owned plant that manufactures household appliances. The plant also has about 18 departments with close to 1,200 workers. Its production process involves two types of manufacturing, one manual and the other automatic. The manual one is now being replaced with technology imported from Italy. The manual-process department previously employed 150 workers, but that number is down to 40 or 50 per shift. Similarly, the number of workers per machine has dropped from five to two. When there are unforeseen increases in demand, temporary workers are hired to meet the extra labor requirements. Most production—close to 90 percent—is for the domestic market, and the rest is under subcontract to a buyer in the United States who packages it and labels it with its trademark.

The firm has reorganized its personnel structure, eliminating six of fifteen job categories. Although temporary workers were fired when the restructuring took place, this job category is still the main door into the firm. Training is done on the job and does not include formal technical education. It amounts to watching what fellow workers do for a few days. Workers are trained to make various items, each of which uses different processes. Changes in the type of item are determined by changes in demand, and for this reason not all machinery is used at the same time. Some workers have been sent to total quality courses, but there are still no groups or circles in which they can participate. To date, quality control is up to a supervisor and a quality control department. Workers are reprimanded when the items they make do not meet specifications. A recent problem in the plant is high employee turnover. According to workers' comments, this is because workers are kept as temporary employees too long; many become impatient with this status and leave. However, permanent employees frequently leave as well.

The firm is in a period of transition in which adopting flexible techniques clashes with established forms of organization and production control. Thus, for example, there is a move to introduce new technology and numerical control machines which reinforce the ability to make product changes easily; however, this move is being made while keeping in place the old features of control and supervision characteristic of mass production. In this sense, the reduction of job categories seems to be more a result of the adoption of new technology than of an overall change in the plant's organizational structure.

Labor is the area that seems to have seen the least progress. Indeed, although Plant B is modernizing its production technology, it has not organized its workers in quality circles, and its command mechanisms are still traditional ones, as are its education and training systems. Therefore, although some workers have been sent to total quality courses, there seems to be no overall plan to bring in the entire flexible production system. Finally, we must note that there is a certain correlation between market orientation and the level of flexible restructuring reached, since the percentage of production for export is much lower in this group of firms than it is for firms in Group A.

As an example of the third group of firms, Group C, we will look at Plant C, with about 800 workers. Production here is still based on traditional assembly lines. Workers get parts they need on a conveyor belt, discard bad pieces, and place usable parts in a box. Although the number of items to be produced is laid out in a work plan, the worker always performs the same task, and quality control takes place at the end of the line. There are no work teams and none of the workers interviewed had taken courses in quality control. Internal labor mobility is practically nonexistent; promotions and job category changes are the exception rather than the rule. Except in the maintenance department, the plant does not have multiskilled workers. In the opinion of the workers interviewed, delays and waste are common. What is interesting is that this plant's parent company has plants in Group A as well, highlighting the marked unevenness in the process of modernization. The contrasts between these firms in Group C and those in Groups

A and B illustrate the deep-going changes that are taking place in production processes, even if they are still far from what production units in the highly industrialized countries are experiencing.

Our interviews with workers allowed us to identify those aspects of the process in which there are conflicts, especially over wages, productivity bonuses, the skill structure, task rotation, and the relationship with supervisors. We began with the hypothesis that a job that gives the worker greater control over his or her productive activity and demands a greater intellectual effort would provide the worker with more satisfaction and a sense of fulfillment, reducing the alienation characteristic of the mechanical systems associated with Fordism and Taylorism. To our surprise, no matter how we asked the question, we could not find this supposed sense of satisfaction which bosses insisted their workers had.

Virtually all workers interviewed complained of low wages, particularly workers at firms in Group A. Their complaints are doubly significant considering that the average minimum wage for all the firms under study is 51.26 percent above the official minimum wage.[46] Salaries are even higher in Group A firms, where the work force is made up entirely of skilled workers whose wage for the lowest job category was close to 32,000 pesos per day in August 1991, or 168.9 percent above minimum wage.

This shows that Mexico's minimum wage is inoperative in practice, at least in industry, where no one works for minimum wage. Nevertheless, the minimum wage continues to be the point of reference in negotiations, functioning as a brake on wage hikes.[47] The fact that the minimum wage is inoperative reflects the considerable lag of wages in Mexico compared to the real value of the labor force. Indeed, the buying power of the minimum wage has been reduced to nearly one-third of its 1982 level (see figure 1). The minimum wage is now 42.5 times its 1982 value, but consumer prices are 124.3 times their level in 1982.[48] Basic necessities for a family of five cost 22,700 pesos in August 1991, nearly two times

---

[46]The official minimum wage was 11,900 pesos per day, while the minimum wage in the firms was 18,000 pesos.

[47]One example that illustrates how the minimum wage is used as a point of reference appears in the *maquiladora* industry in Mexico's northern border region. In the Japanese *maquiladoras* in Tijuana that produce electronic products, workers start at minimum wage and receive monthly bonuses thereafter for up to six months, when wages level off. Given the area's high turnover rates, most workers never earn much above the minimum. In one plant I visited, 40 percent of the work force had been employed for less than six months (author interview with the personnel director of the Sony plant in Tijuana, March 16, 1992).

[48]The data on wages were taken from a report presented by the Taller de Análisis Económico de la UNAM, August 1991.

the minimum wage, and this only covered essential consumer goods—not education, clothing, recreation, etc. Therefore, just to reach 1982 conditions, wages should be increased by 193 percent. Given this figure, even firms with the highest wages are paying multiskilled workers several thousand pesos less than what the worst-paid worker received in 1982.[49]

A significant point about workers' wage levels is the fact that very few of the managers interviewed knew what the minimum and maximum wages were for workers in their plants. Management sees labor as just one more cost, and this distances managers from the real problems their employees face. For a manager it was enough to know that the firm's wages were above the minimum.

Aside from low wages, there is another, less obvious factor that explains the dissatisfaction among workers employed in the firms with the best wages. It is the issue of compensation during transition: workers in factories that are modernizing are aware of the productivity increase and feel that this increase is not reflected in their wages. The tendency to eliminate job categories, lay off helpers, and rotate tasks is perceived by workers as additional work and responsibility that is not sufficiently rewarded. As we shall see, the problem of compensation is a very complex one, since managers and directors frequently follow the recommendations of personnel management specialists, who advise them to avoid economic rewards and instead grant acknowledgments, diplomas, prizes, etc. However, any noneconomic reward system would have to have as its starting point a base wage that workers consider to be fair. Fourteen years of continuously depressed wages in Mexico are a heavy drag on the development of a new form of wage relation.

In general terms, the problem of wages is so important that some economists believe that the crisis of the Taylorist and Fordist models is a crisis of the wage relation (Boyer 1990; Hualde and Micheli 1988), which includes the structure of job classifications and the process of wage formation. These are precisely the most sensitive factors for workers in firms that have been or are being restructured.

The problem consists in knowing how to determine wages in the process of educating multiskilled workers and redefining wage categories and work assignments. This factor is at the center of possible modifications to Mexican labor legislation. Establishing new mechanisms for wage formation takes on special importance

---

[49]The U.S. minimum wage of $4.25 per hour equals a day's work for a minimum-wage Mexican worker. Minimum wages in Europe range between six and twenty-two times higher than the Mexican minimum wage; and minimum wages throughout Latin America tend to be significantly higher than Mexico's (Taller de Análisis Económico de la UNAM).

in the framework of the gradual dismantling of worker protections that were previously in place in Mexico. Several studies present evidence of a gradual loss of union presence in collective bargaining over working conditions, resulting in an increase in the prerogatives of management in areas that were traditionally under union control (Zapata 1992a; Quintero 1990; Middlebrook 1991).

Boyer (1987) believes that wages must be viewed in light of their relationship to monetary and fiscal policy; the positive fiscal effects of slow wage gains must be combined with an expansive budget policy. However, this optimal combination is far removed from the situation in Mexico, where wages have moved drastically downward and budget policy is far from expansive. Through state-society economic agreements (the PSE until 1988, followed by the Pact for Stability and Economic Growth, PECE), the state has used wages to bring about deflation.

Although they have not completely come to grips with the problem of job classifications and rewards, the Monterrey firms have tried different compensation mechanisms. One is corrective action teams, made up of engineers and workers who share ideas on how to improve productivity, quality, and capacity. When the team is able to lower costs, they are awarded prizes (medals or watches, for example), and some members are promoted. But even in this case workers complain that the distribution of prizes and promotions is controlled by the superintendent, since there are no established objective criteria for winning them. Hence this kind of compensation tends to generate conflicts, resentment, and disappointment. The most modern firms have introduced bonuses for demonstrated knowledge (determined through an evaluation), and some firms are trying to include supervisory personnel in this system. Here too the goal is to have multiskilled employees who rotate through various departments, but the problem is precisely that they have not found an adequate compensation system.

Worker discontent caused by the lack of fair rewards does not seem to have channels for collective expression, precisely because of the white unions which predominate in these firms. The only way to express dissatisfaction with the wage and labor regime is to leave the firm. In response to our questionnaires, management pointed to high turnover as one of the main obstacles to adopting flexible production. Although several factors may interact to generate turnover rates, the law of supply and demand in the labor market has begun to operate.

How the labor market works in Monterrey varies by type of employee: the highest personnel turnover occurs among unskilled workers, who do not remain in the firm long enough to receive training or get into a higher job category.[50] This fact, along with the growing demand for skilled employees, has produced a scarcity of technicians and skilled workers, and their wages have begun to rise as a result.[51] While this might seem to support the private sector's assertion that wage increases will come on their own according to the laws of the market, the cost of starting workers out at a very low wage may turn out to be high for industry by producing a costly period of high employee turnover. In fact this has begun to affect training programs. The immediate effect is that skilled workers join the pool of those who rotate from one firm to another. In this sense, the supposed savings from an inexpensive labor force may be counterproductive in the medium term by retarding the leveling out of Mexican workers' training and productivity indexes.

According to managers, the high employee turnover rates in Monterrey are due to changes in the culture of work among the new generation and to the lack of government control over the informal economy, which makes it more profitable to work at street crossings than in factories. Managers believe that the government should suppress these informal activities. In this sense, they view the growth of the informal economy—not low wages—as the cause of their difficulty in keeping workers. But as we saw earlier, the workers hold a different opinion: most of them need two or three wages in the household in order to survive; a single-wage family faces serious hardships. Extra income can supplement an inadequate wage.

The mechanisms for wage formation that develop in Mexico in the future could either accelerate or retard change. These mechanisms are directly related to the skill structure and its rewards. As we were able to observe, most of the firms studied have reduced job categories on average from sixteen to nine, and there are cases where categories were reduced from twenty-two to only six. We also found that the temporary worker category is becoming a less certain entryway into a firm. While temporary workers used to become permanent employees after a certain time period, the new tendency is to hire additional labor when demand rises, with no company commitment for long-term employment. These measures have been implemented so far without any organized resistance from the workers. Although workers do not welcome these changes—since they increase the intensity and responsibility of their jobs with no corresponding increase in compensation—they

---

[50] According to some personnel directors interviewed. At Metalsa, for example, most workers who leave the firm do so in the first six months.

[51] One worker pointed out that a competing firm was trying to recruit specialized workers by going to their homes with offers of higher wages.

lack the means to express their discontent through collective action.

The move toward flexible production has produced two noteworthy outcomes. First, the benefits are visibly one-sided, accruing to capital, which could lead to serious conflicts in the near future. Second, there is a clear contradiction between the changes this process brings to the forms of organizing production and the persistence of the old framework governing labor relations in the firms. However, the characteristics of the trade unionism that prevails in these industries have so far made it possible for management to introduce these changes unilaterally without any organized resistance, as we shall see in the next section.

TRADE UNIONISM IN MONTERREY GROUP FIRMS

For sixty years the large Monterrey firms have had white unions, characterized by close ties to the company. They are unlike either official unions or left-wing unions. In his study of white unions in Monterrey Group firms, Javier Rojas (1983: 85–104) describes the essential characteristics that define this form of organization: The unions' ideological principles are drawn from the social doctrine of the Catholic church, which puts a conciliatory stamp on their relationship with the company and distances them from the state and political parties, as well as from other Mexican trade unions.[52] They declare themselves independent and autonomous of the company, the state, and political parties (although their autonomy with regard to the company can easily be called into question). They defend private property, which they believe is the "incentive to work and the firm foundation for personal dignity and independence, and what gives the worker's family stability." Union activity revolves around economic demands based on the labor contract, and strikes are discarded as a method of struggle.[53] In short, white union practices can be summarized as collaboration with the company and negotiation instead of strikes and/or violent forms of resistance.

---

[52]José Ortiz Bernal, one of the founders of the Cuauhtémoc and Famosa workers' union (from which the other white unions developed), defines the organization's doctrine and principles thus: "In this era of degrading materialism, it is time to reaffirm the philosophy that has always inspired this union . . . the principles and postulates of *Christian humanism*" (Rojas 1983: 85).

[53]The National Federation of Independent Trade Unions (FENSI), which includes most Monterrey Group unions, declares in its statement of principles: "our trade union experience shows that it has been possible to raise the standard of living of the working class without resorting to violent and destructive methods, because the struggle for the rule of social justice is carried out by legal and rationally necessary procedures which guarantee and increase workers' advances without damaging collective welfare."

The direct consequence of this type of trade union organization is a lack of union control over conditions of work. In contrast to official trade unions and unions with a greater degree of autonomy, white unions have never negotiated a contract that included an entry clause, which grants the union preference in filling job openings, vacancies, and promotions (Rojas 1983; Vellinga 1981).[54] Nor do they have an exclusion clause, which requires that the company fire any worker expelled from the union.

Lacking these powerful instruments and any capacity to prevent firings and defend job security, white unions become mere tools of the company, serving only to assure compliance with labor law. Monterrey Group firms guarantee the permanence of this type of unionism by maintaining strong control over the workers through a paternalistic system which includes benefits surpassing those required by law and keeps a strict lookout for any sign of dissidence or opposition to management or union actions. The mere suspicion that a worker has ties to a left-wing organization results in the worker's immediate firing and his or her name being reported to all area firms through blacklists drawn up by the Nuevo León Employers' Center (CPNL). A similar fate awaits workers who become involved in labor disputes.[55]

Because the prevalence of white unions in the Monterrey firms eased the introduction of flexible production, these companies have not had to face the problems that other Mexican firms encounter when seeking to reduce the power of the union within their plants.[56] In fact, the current debate over modifying Mexico's Federal Labor Law in order to adapt it to this new form of production seems to repeat the old quarrel between the Cuauhtémoc group and the federal government in 1929, when the 1931 labor law was being discussed, but this time conditions favor the employers. It was in the heat of the 1929 discussions that the Business Federation of Mexico (COPARMEX) was founded to protect the private sector from state efforts to control relations between capital and labor within firms (Rojas 1983). The main points of the law

---

[54]For example, the contract at Hylsa, the main company of the Alfa group, states: "The firm shall select and hire the personnel it needs to do the work it requires, whether on a temporary or permanent basis, with the understanding that new hires must join the union before starting to work in the company. The worker shall have twenty-four hours after signing the contract to do this" (1977 Hylsa contract, quoted in Rojas 1983). The contracts at Cydsa, Cervecería Cuauhtémoc, Vidriera, and Crisa have similar clauses.

[55]Statement by a worker fired from one of these companies, quoted in Rojas 1983. The existence of lists drawn up by the CPNL was corroborated in an author interview with a personnel manager.

[56]Studies carried out in the automobile industry (Middlebrook 1991; Carrillo 1990) and in the *maquiladoras* (Quintero 1991, 1992; Gambrill 1990; Carrillo 1985, 1988) indicate the Mexican unions' increasing loss of power.

which incensed the private sector were: labor contracts for unde-
fined periods; having to pay three months of wages to fired
workers; granting the union the authority to name personnel
under the exclusion clause; the conditions that justified a strike;
and state arbitration through the Conciliation and Arbitration
Boards (Rojas 1983; Vellinga 1981). All of these are at issue once
again.

It is no coincidence that the first white union was formed in
1931, the year the labor law was enacted.[57] Apparently employers
were able to include some points in the labor code that allowed for
white unions, even though the spirit of the law favored the
formation of corporatist unions and union control over conditions
of employment. Articles 154 and 395 of the Federal Labor Law are
particularly significant. Article 154 states that if there is a contract
and if it has an entry clause, preference in occupying vacancies or
newly created jobs will be determined by what is established in the
contract and the union bylaws. Complementing this, Article 395
states that it *may* be established in the contract that the employer
will take as workers only those who are members of the contracting
union. These articles make union control over hiring contingent on
negotiations between the union and the company; in other words,
negotiating control over hiring into any given contract depends on
the union's strength and autonomy. In the case of white unions,
management retains this prerogative.

The Monterrey Group's struggle to protect their unions from
state co-optation and left-wing influences seems about to end.
Employers seem to be fighting their last battle in the field of labor
legislation. Business organizations led by the CPNL have made a
series of proposals to modify the law; so far these have been
rejected by the Labor Congress even though these proposals reflect
the situation which de facto already prevails in most Mexican
industries.

In general, the Monterrey Group firms seek a flexible workday,
hourly wages, and fewer restrictions on hiring and firing. The
CPNL's proposal hinges on modifying Article 123 of the Mexican
Constitution (see appendix 4) to make the 48-hour workweek
adaptable to variations in demand, eliminating overtime pay when
large orders must be met and doing away with dead time once the
weekly quota set by the demand has been met. In other words, a
worker could work for more than eight hours a day early in the
week and be sent home the rest of the week once he or she had met

---

[57]The Unión de Trabajadores Cuauhtémoc y Famosa was established in 1931 in
the Cervecería Cuauhtémoc and Famosa companies.

the obligatory forty-eight hours. Only hours above and beyond that weekly total would be considered overtime.

As a necessary complement to this new distribution of the workweek, pay would be calculated hourly (not daily as is now done). A base minimum wage would be set for the entire country (there now are several minimum wage regions based on differences in the cost of living), and professional minimum wages would be eliminated. This would tie wages to demonstrated skills. Finally, as in the COPARMEX proposal, the CPNL proposal seeks to undo the current constitutional restrictions on firing workers by limiting employers' responsibility.

Both proposals—that of the Nuevo León Employers' Center and that of the COPARMEX—reflect the new demands for making wages and hours of work more flexible. However, they avoid the issues of reskilling and the organization of work; introducing these topics would mean opening up the debate about the mechanisms of wage formation linked to increases in workers' skills and the firms' increases in productivity.

Spokespersons for employers indicated that companies want to bring labor legislation up to date, adapt it to the demands of flexible production, and prevent it from limiting the firms' international competitiveness. However, the proposals of both employer groups virtually eliminate all worker protections by doing away with guarantees of secure employment, limiting recourse to strikes, and reducing the employers' responsibilities to employees. This leaves many important issues to be negotiated between the parties, which presupposes their equality, something that does not yet exist in Mexico.

It is not surprising that the Labor Congress has rejected the proposals. What is surprising is the inability of trade unions to present a viable counterproposal which could open up the debate around the configuration of the new wage relation that the country requires. The proposals circulated by one sector of the official trade unions do not address the underlying issues; they gloss over the transformations at work in the labor and trade union sphere and limit themselves to traditional petitions of an economic nature. For their part, the white unions in FENSI (see note 53) or the recently formed Federation of Workers in Autonomous Trade Unions (FTSA) do not even have a document outlining their position toward the changes that have taken place within the firms.

The short-term risks, but potentially long-term gains, of a company's unilateral introduction of flexible production measures to regulate work were made clear in the case of the Ford Cuautitlán plant, where a serious labor dispute arose as a result. The 61-day strike was to protest the way in which the company implemented its modernization program in 1987, when the old labor contract expired. The company broke the strike by temporarily closing the plant and firing all workers. The plant later reopened and rehired 2,500 of the original workers, but on the company's terms (*El Porvenir*, June 4, 1991).

Apparently this strategy benefited the company; the firm was able to introduce the flexible mechanisms and it became a model of productivity in the Mexican automobile industry. In 1988, its engine department won the Q-1 award, and in 1989 the foundry department won the same award. However, the measures introduced by the company with the support of the Confederation of Mexican Workers (CTM)—including reducing job categories from sixteen to only six and setting up task rotation—were viewed as threatening by many workers. Raúl Escobar, leader of the dissidents who challenged the company's project, said they "pushed the union aside and established a unilateral work relationship in which the company imposes practically everything." Task rotation is suspect because "it allows the company to change a worker's job without the worker being able to say no or demand additional pay" (*El Porvenir*, July 25, 1991).

The dissidents tried to decertify the CTM and affiliate with the Revolutionary Labor Federation (COR). The dispute severely impacted the production process, with a drastic decline in quality and productivity. The CTM retained the union contract in July 1991 after a vote recount that had to be held under the eyes of several hundred uniformed police, dogs, plainclothesmen, and federal agents (*El Porvenir*, June 25, 1991).

An alliance between the company, the state, and the CTM to facilitate the introduction of flexible contracts and working conditions clearly carries with it the risk of closing down the channels for workers to express their discontent. Until now this has resulted in two types of response: in firms where workers have a tradition of collective action, organized dissidence has sometimes affected productivity gains. In new firms, with little or no union tradition, discontent is apparently released through high employee turnover. The latter has become a serious problem in some auto and electronics plants located in the border region, where turnover can reach 30 percent a year (Shaiken 1990).

The transition from Fordism to new forms of organizing production (sometimes called Toyotism) is not a mechanical process, nor is it the only alternative. The new technology can coexist with various models of work organization and labor relations. The tendency toward flexible production can take place without the responsible and autonomous participation of workers, but it irreversibly affects working conditions—wages, job security, and the length of the workday—especially when the starting point is that introducing flexible production requires reducing union control over working conditions. Employer demands regarding changes in the Federal Labor Law seem to stem from this point of view, since they are mainly aimed at eliminating the entry and exclusion, subcontracting, job mobility, definition of tasks, and conflict resolution clauses, among others.

Thus, white unionism appears as an attractive option to employers since it also excludes state intervention. However, our interviews uncovered signs of discontent among workers, who perceive task rotation, quality monitoring, and layoffs of helpers as increased responsibility for themselves, for which they are not sufficiently rewarded.

This is not a case of new firms and inexperienced workers, but of an entire bargaining and control structure based on a system of benefits and loyalties designed for the old forms of organization of the work process. In this system, job security and promotions based on seniority played an important role. However, the retraining programs that are being developed are aimed primarily at young workers. In our interviews, some workers with high seniority expressed fear about the changes that are taking place, since they do not know how they will be affected. This means that the white unions in the Monterrey firms are no guarantee of labor stability given changing working conditions.

Furthermore, top management itself believes that one of the greatest obstacles to incorporating flexible production techniques is the difficulty of superimposing new mechanisms on an organizational structure that is already in operation. Efforts to develop new relationships of work, of negotiation, and of contracting may meet similar resistance and generate similar problems.

6

Conclusion

By the end of the 1980s, the Monterrey Group firms clearly fore-shadowed the shape that Mexico's new insertion in the international economy will take. The economic opening, which in its simplest form involved opening the doors to foreign investment and stimulating exports of Mexican products, is a much richer and more complex process, in which the forms of association between national and foreign capital and the relationships between firms within and outside Mexican territory are unleashing deep-going transformations and driving the modernization of Mexican industry.

However, what is less clear is the place that Mexico will occupy in the new international order. The case of Monterrey undermines the explanatory value of theories based on a new international division of labor (NIDL) in which countries of the periphery are assigned labor-intensive and less-skilled industrial activities. While the increasing spread of *maquiladoras* in Third World countries seems to confirm the NIDL hypothesis, the establishment of high-technology automobile plants in Mexico, as well as the interest on the part of large U.S. and European transnational companies in locating their plants in Mexico, introduce nuances in the explanation. Even more important, how should we interpret the movement of Mexican capital toward developed countries?[58] The cases of two companies analyzed here, Vitro and Cemex, which acquired large firms in the United States and Spain, might seem to go against the logic of comparative advantage for countries with low wage costs. At the same time, associations between capitals

---

[58] We must distinguish between the forms of investment carried out by firms as expansion strategies and capital flight to the United States and Europe, carried out by private parties seeking a haven for their savings in times of crisis. Capital flight reached very elevated levels in Latin America over the last two decades.

are not only one-way, center-periphery movements. Most of the coinvestments analyzed show an exchange of equal numbers of shares between the Mexican firm and the foreign firm with which it forms a partnership. In other words, large Mexican industries seek to become a part of the same globalizing strategies and forms of capital expansion that are currently taking place in the industrialized countries.

Along with opening up an entire new field of research on the effects of capital expansion from the periphery to the center, these facts show that the criteria for capital investment go beyond the cost factor to include a series of elements related to global market strategies, as well as other factors such as public policies, technology strategies, and the extent of worker unionization. In this sense, the thesis of the regulation school (Marglin 1974; Glyn, Hughes, Lipietz, Singh 1988) is correct in emphasizing the importance of the macro-economic structure, the production system, and the rules for coordinating a given international order. In other words, each country's institutional arrangements and the way in which these direct the country's relationship with the international order are determining factors.

Therefore, in spite of the undeniable influence of neoliberal discourse in defining Mexico's new development model, the role of the state becomes crucial. The case of Monterrey shows that so far the state holds the reins of change, despite its sale of important parastatal firms and its concessions to the business sector. In this context, NAFTA takes on singular importance for the Mexican government, since it represents the Mexican state's proposal not only to its future partners but to the world regarding the place Mexico hopes to occupy in the international arena. Moreover, the country's proximity to the United States has awakened the interest of Europe and Japan in the results of this agreement, while Latin America watches attentively, hoping for similar trade agreements with other countries of the hemisphere. Despite the fact that Mexico was at a clear disadvantage in the negotiations, NAFTA appears to be the best option for consolidating the modernizing project, from the point of view of the government.

Its new alliance with the business sector has given the government important support to push forward this proposal, with big business spearheading the process. Thus, the Mexican experience, and in particular the case of Monterrey, make clear the interdependence of state and capital, even in a period of economic liberalism. The state seeks to reaffirm its sovereignty by encouraging a strong national industry which can compete in international markets. This is why economic opening and deregulation were accompanied by a series of policies designed to support and strengthen large industry, without which much of this sector might not have survived the 1982 crisis. These same policies prepare firms to face the total deregulation that comes with the signing of NAFTA.[59]

While there is no guarantee that Mexican capital will not leave the country if conditions are adverse to it remaining, it is easier for the government to establish alliances with national capital than with international capital. This is because the former will tend to concentrate greater influence and power in Mexican territory, precisely because of the support they receive from the state apparatus of their own country. Although this may vary considerably as firm size increases, the fact that most large corporations from industrialized countries keep their decision-making centers in their place of origin, regardless of their degree of globalization, backs this view.

In Mexico, the Vitro case seems to confirm this. Under its globalizing strategies, 60 percent of its assets and 50 percent of its sales are outside of Mexico. Nevertheless, Vitro continues to consider itself a Mexico-based firm, as stated by its general director:

> Vitro is a company that began in Mexico, has grown in Mexico, and is headquartered in Mexico. Vitro is determined to continue to pull its weight and help the country grow and develop. I want Mexican purchasing power to increase, and I want a truly better country (*El Financiero Internacional*, April 6, 1992).

The profitability of each type of capital tends to depend increasingly on its ability to influence state policies. In this sense, we could draw the preliminary conclusion that the proclaimed "slimming of the Mexican state" and its withdrawal from the role of entrepreneur in important areas of economic activity do not necessarily point toward less intervention in the economy, but rather toward a new type of intervention involving a new alliance between capital and the state.

At this point we should ask ourselves what effects this project will have inside Mexico. Will it really result in productive linkages and generalized modernization, or will it give rise to increasing polarization and impoverishment (De la Garza 1992; Roldán 1992)? What will the new social pact look like? Without trying to answer these questions, we can reflect on what the case of Monterrey tells

---

[59]The concertation mechanism, which has been employed in Mexico since 1987 as a means for setting economic policy guidelines, illustrates how state intervention was needed to restrict the free play of forces in the economy which otherwise would have led to hyperinflation.

us in this regard and draw some conclusions about what is happening inside the plants and the effects in the country as a whole.

The reorganization of work in Monterrey firms faithfully follows the new paradigm of industrial production. The firms' determination to reduce both inventory and waste to a minimum has led to modifications in technology and forms of management which have important consequences for labor relations within firms. In general, the features of this process are positive, if by positive we understand a push forward which allows the country to exit the crisis and correct its international isolation brought on by corruption, the lack of democracy, technological backwardness, and productive inefficiency. The positive aspects are the entry of leading-edge technology, the installation of new and modern plants, access to more efficient forms of production organization, and increased trade, not only with the United States but also with Europe and Japan. But the process also has negative features, understood as everything that implies the concentration of power and economic resources in an elite, to the detriment of the workers and broad sectors of the population.

Technological reconversion in the Monterrey firms has been very important. However, it is hard to determine from these case studies how widespread this process is in Mexico. Although the firms studied are heterogeneous in terms of the products they manufacture, the companies share two important elements: Given that they belong to the Monterrey Group, management boards contain members of the same families. This guarantees a certain unity and homogeneity in expansion and technological investment policies, just like it unified the strategies followed by the firms to exit the crisis. Second, these firms are the historical result of a process of vertical and horizontal integration developed over the last one hundred years, so that many of them were and still are each others' main suppliers; this aspect, as we saw, is singularly important in the process of technology transfer.

Nevertheless, there are some factors that are not inherent to the Monterrey Group that largely determine the characteristics of Mexico's technological development. First, investment in technology is driven by changes in government policy aimed at reducing traditionally protectionist mechanisms, opening up trade, and eliminating subsidies, as well as signing the NAFTA with the United States and Canada. In this sense, the process of economic opening acts as a continuing stimulus to technological investment, given the need to adapt products to the requirements of international markets. Opposed to this factor for change, however, are the fact that most production is still oriented toward an internal market that does not yet justify costly technological investment and the difficulties in technology transfer that result from insufficient infrastructure and a shortage of qualified personnel to operate it.

Second, change is driven by firms' exposure to new philosophies of quality and the presence of Japanese, European, and U.S. consultants. This results in the development of education and training courses in the new production and flexible management techniques. Opposed to these elements are confusion between the new and old forms of management and planning, a resistance to change, and above all the lack of systematic thinking about how to adapt the models to the country's conditions. In other words, contact with international firms and markets is introducing elements of change that combine in a peculiar way with features already in place.

The linkages established thus far through supplier networks do not seem to extend to small and mid-sized industrial sectors. The demands of JIT operations are beyond the reach of small and mid-sized firms which have minimal access to financial resources, to technical and market knowledge, and to the information needed for company reconversion. In this sense, the Monterrey firms are pursuing a new type of vertical and horizontal integration to ensure quality of inputs among themselves. In developed countries this kind of integration has been discarded in favor of subcontracting. In Monterrey, the only form of subcontracting we found is related to secondary services, those not directly related to the manufacturing process (janitorial and food services, personnel transport, etc.). Although this may change in the future, the current situation points to the nearly insurmountable difficulties that small and mid-sized firms face for building production linkages. If we add to this the enormous share that large industries represent of total value added in their sector (71.8 percent in 1988) and of personnel employed (49.4 percent) (De la Garza 1992), we might well conclude that what is taking shape in Mexico is a highly polarized system.

On the other hand, the case of the Monterrey firms hardly confirms the optimistic vision of restructuring as stimulating "harmonious and cooperative relations and high skill levels that would assure efficient and quality production" (Roldán 1992: 2). What we find is the unilateral introduction of flexible approaches with collaborationist trade union support, bringing wage controls and suppressing all opposition. The presence of white unions gave Monterrey an advantage over other firms of the same size in the restructuring process since the Monterrey firms did not have to relocate to areas with less of a union tradition. The Monterrey Group was able to draw on a sizable pool of experienced and trained workers laid off during the crisis. Thus, despite personnel adjustments, unemployment in Monterrey decreased noticeably at the end of the 1980s as a result of industrial expansion.

The unilateral introduction of flexible programs is not just the policy of the Monterrey firms. It is also the current government's labor policy, aimed at adapting labor relations to the requirements of the new world organization of labor. Control over the labor force is gaining tremendous importance internationally in the competition to attract industrial investment (Gertler 1988; Micheli 1991). This is occurring because the labor factor seems to be one of the weaknesses of the new model of production organization. There are three reasons for this: First, just-in-time production and the tendency to eliminate inventories make firms highly vulnerable to any stoppage in production resulting from a union dispute. Second, the introduction of new technologies tends to create a segment of highly skilled workers whose education and training make them very valuable to the firm and at the same time give them greater power within it. Third, the globalization of production may give rise to transnational forms of worker organization.

Taylorism developed precisely to control the only nonuniform factor in mass production, human labor. When breaking with this system through the introduction of flexible forms of production, some of this control is lost. In Mexico, the increased company prerogatives and the unions' loss of power over working conditions are generalized trends (De la Garza 1992). Zapata (1992a: 2) points to a series of indicators of unions' loss of control in the workplace: the union loses its say in vertical and horizontal mobility, and its capacity for collective representation is weakened.

The white unions are also affected. The structure for negotiation and control in this form of unionism is based on a system of benefits and loyalties designed to fit the old forms of organization of the work process. In this system job security and promotions based on seniority played an important role. By making training and not seniority the driving force of vertical mobility, and by replacing the system of steady jobs with the company's option to rotate workers from one task to another, the pact established between employers and workers is modified de facto, undermining the union's credibility. In other words, white unionism in its current form does not necessarily represent the alternative model of unionism that the country needs, not even from the employers' point of view. Despite its autonomy from the state and its collaboration with firms, white unionism is immersed in the national schema of labor relations based on corporatism and Mexico's social pact.

Indeed, although the state has made it easier for firms to introduce flexibility by recurring to the Ministry of Labor and the

Conciliation and Arbitration Boards to suppress union resistance, the currency of the social pact is expressed in the survival of the system of social health benefits (IMSS, ISSSTE), housing (INFON-AVIT), and in the fact that the Federal Labor Law has not been changed. President Salinas decided not to carry out a deep-going restructuring of the corporatist pact, apparently for political reasons (Zapata 1992b).

However, the question remains whether this stance can be maintained once NAFTA enters into operation. Witness the pressure exerted on the Canadian government to eliminate a series of benefits and social programs because U.S. firms viewed them as disloyal trade practices (*Action Canada Network*, June 1992). Once NAFTA goes into effect it will necessarily eliminate the price and wage controls established in the Pact for Stability and Economic Growth. In an apparent effort to buy time, the current administration is undermining the bases of the corporatist system by weakening the corporations that created it, on the one hand, and on the other, maintaining the social welfare institutions that sealed the old pact.

The weakening of corporatism places the issue of worker representation on the agenda. For the labor sector, it is essential to guarantee workers' representation in both the country's workplace and political life. Labor's influence in Mexico's political arena used to be exerted within the framework of corporatism and the alliance with the state. While this meant a significant loss of autonomy, the labor sector gained a form of political representation that negotiated its most general interests and achieved essential conquests vis-à-vis the state and employers, largely reflected in the Federal Labor Law. Given the absence of a labor party or strong, autonomous trade unions, breaking the corporatist relationship at this time would leave workers at a severe disadvantage. On the other hand, the increasing union bureaucratism resulting from corporatism seriously affected workers' representation in the workplace. This is reflected not only in a failure to enforce labor law, but also in the absence of mechanisms to address specific worker demands. The lack of union democracy divorced workers from their leaders, fostering corruption and union posts held for life.

This contradiction is at the center of stymied efforts to improve labor relations in Mexico. The leaders of the most advanced sectors of trade unionism recognize the need to join the discussion on modernization and productivity (*Trabajo* 1 [1989]; *El Norte*, May 1, 1993). However, such negotiations within the plant require a representative union organization that can speak for all the workers if the union's proposal is to carry any weight.

From the employers' point of view, the legal forms set in the Federal Labor Law and the traditional forms of collective contracts hinder the implementation of the new forms for organizing production that their firms need if they are to become competitive. Therefore, even though Monterrey employers have white unions, they have spearheaded radical proposals to change labor law, demanding totally flexible labor relations. "Flexible" as applied to labor relations refers specifically to job descriptions, length of the workday, worker mobility between tasks, and forms of hiring and firing; all these elements would enable managers to adapt to changing demand and to handle workers so as to increase production efficiency and cut costs. Since the entire system of worker protections rests on the aspects that employers want to transform, an agreement is obviously not easy to achieve.

In summary, we can say that the Monterrey firms present a panorama of change in the context of a restructuring of the industrial production system on a world scale and in the framework of profound contradictions unleashed by Mexico's process of modernization. Newly introduced forms of work organization clash with the corporatist structure of labor relations defined not only in the Federal Labor Law but in the very relationships between the state and organized labor. Moreover, innovations in equipment and forms of management also run up against problems with regard to service infrastructure, the availability of appropriate raw materials, and the lack of qualified personnel, as well as resistance from old forms of command. At the same time, a shortage of dependable national suppliers slows down the introduction of the just-in-time system, leading to incomplete adoptions of the Japanese and European models of flexible production and limiting the participation of small and mid-sized industries in export circuits.

However, economic opening has already brought important modifications in Mexico's relations with First World countries. A segment of industry has developed that can not only compete in international markets but even expand its industries and capitals to developed countries. The state's role in this entire process and its new alliance with employers are decisive. Nevertheless, it is still unclear what place other social sectors will occupy in the emerging social pact. The difficult political situation in Mexico, the crawling pace of political reform, and the approaching change in administration all help explain why concerted efforts have been made to keep certain social programs alive. Since these underlying factors are temporary in nature, what we see as continuity in social welfare programs held over from the old social pact may also give way.

Appendix 1

Composition of the
Industrial Groups

Firm	Activity	Location
ALFA INDUSTRIAL GROUP		
Hylsa	Iron & steel	Monterrey,N.L.
		Xotla,Pue.
		Las Encinas, Col.
		Colima, Col.
		México, D.F.
		Guadalajara, Jal.
Aceros Planos	Iron & steel	Monterrey, N.L.
Galvak	Iron & steel	Monterrey, N.L.
Atlas	Iron & steel	Apizaco, Tlax.
Cía. Metalúrgica México	Iron & steel	
Las Encinas	Mining	Colima, Col.
Papel y Embarques	Wood products	Monterrey, N.L.
Empaques de Cartón Titanic	Paper & cellulose	Monterrey, N.L.
Akra 1	Textiles	Monterrey, N.L.
		Tampico, Tamps.
Akra 2	Textiles	Santa Catarina, N.L.
Akra 3	Textiles	Edo. Méx.
Megatek	Electrical machinery & equipment	Monterrey, N.L.
Fud Alimentos y Subsidiarios	Food	
Nemak	Autoparts	Villa de García, N.L.
Petrocel	Petrochemicals	Tampico, Tamps.
		México, D.F.
Polioles	Petrochemicals	Guadalajara, Jal.
Acojinamientos Selther	Other manufac. activities	Monterrey, N.L.
Indelpro	Polypropylene	Altamira, Tamps.
Alfa Industrias	Services	Monterrey, N.L.
Casolar	Services	Garza García, N.L.
Corporación Hylsa	Services	Monterrey, N.L.
Dinámica	Services	Monterrey, N.L.
Ormak	Services	Monterrey, N.L.
Fracc. Hotelera del Pacífico	Hotels & restaurants	

Firm	Activity	Location
CEMEX INDUSTRIAL GROUP		
Cementos Mexicanos	Cement	Monterrey, N.L.
		Torreón, Coah.
		Valles, San Luis Potosí
		Huichapan, Hgo.
Cementos Atoyac	Cement	Puebla, Pue.
Cementos Guadalajara	Cement	Guadalajara, Jal.
		Ensenada, BCN
Cementos Maya	Cement	Mérida, Yuc.
		León, Guanajuato
Cementos Anáhuac	Cement	Barrientos, Edo. Méx.
		Tamuín, S.L.P.
Cementos del Yaqui	Cement	Hermosillo, Son.
Cementos Portland Nac.	Cement	Hermosillo, Son.
Cementos Sinaloa	Cement	El Fuerte, Sin.
Cementos Tolteca	Cement	Atotonilco, Hgo.
		Tula, Hgo.
		Zapoltilic, Jal.
Cemex Firms Abroad		
Sunbelt Enterprises	Cement	Houston, Tex.
Texas Sunbelt	Sales	Corpus Christi, Tex.
Houston Shell and Concrete	Concrete	Houston, Tex.
Houston Concrete Products	Concrete	Houston, Tex.
Sunward Materials	Cement	Arizona & New Mexico
Pacific Coast Cement	Cement	Los Angeles, California
C.L. Pharris	Cement	Los Angeles, California
Aggregate Transportation	Sales	Phoenix, Arizona
Southwestern Sunbelt Cement	Sales	Casas Grandes, Arizona
		Phoenix, Arizona
		El Paso, Tex.
		Albuquerque, New
		Mexico
		El Centro, California
		National City, California
Valencia	Cement	Spain
Sansón	Cement	Spain
CYDSA INDUSTRIAL GROUP		
Celulosa y Derivados	Fibers	Monterrey, N.L.
Rayón	Rayon cord	Monterrey, N.L.
Crysel	Acrylic fiber	El Salto, Jal.
Derivados Acrílicos	Acrylic threads	San Luis Potosí, S.L.P.
Propirey	Polypropylene film	Monterrey, N.L.
Celorey	Cellophane film	Monterrey, N.L.
Celloprint	Cellophane film	México, D.F.
Reyprint	Printing & laminating	Monterrey, N.L.
Colombin Bel	Polyurethane foam	México, D.F.
Policid	Vinyl polychloride	La Presa, Edo. Méx.
		Altamira, Tamps.
Plásticos Rex	PVC tubing	México, D.F.
		Monterrey, N.L.
		Guadalajara, Jal.
Plásticos Laminados	Plastic cloth	Edo. Méx.

Firm	Activity	Location
Bonlam	Nonwoven cloth	San Luis Potosí, S.L.P.
Industrias Cydsa Bayer	Toluen-di-isocyanate	México, D.F. Coatzacoalcos, Ver.
Industrias Químicas	Chloride & caustic soda	México, D.F. Monterrey, N.L.
Plantas Químicas	Chemical products	Monterrey, N.L.
Novaquim	Rubber-based chemicals & antioxidants	México, D.F. Altamira, Tamps.
Quimobásicos	Propellant gases	Monterrey, N.L. Mexicali, BCN
Sales del Istmo	Edible/industrial salts	Coatzacoalcos, Ver.
Servicio y Tratamiento de Aguas	Water service/treatment	Monterrey, N.L.
Central Cydsa	Real estate	Monterrey, N.L.
Consorcio Intermex	Foreign trade	Monterrey, N.L.

IMSA INDUSTRIAL GROUP

Firm	Activity	Location
Imsa Signode	Steel	Ciénega de Flores, N.L.
Industrias Monterrey	Steel	San Nicolás de los Garza, N.L.
Aceros Planos	Steel	Monterrey, N.L.
Cubiertas Metálicas	Metal products	
Muebles Alfa	Metal products	Garza García, N.L.
Productos Infantiles Alfa	Metal products	Santa Catarina, N.L.
Robertson Mexicana	Metal products	Monterrey, N.L.
Stabilit	Metal products	México, D.F.
Vigacero Imsa	Metal products	
Acumuladores Mexicanos	Batteries	Monterrey, N.L.
Acumuladores del Centro	Batteries	Tlaxcala, Tlax.
	Sales	
Láminas y Productos Especiales	Sales	
Morvik Proveedora	Sales	
Tracto Victoria	Sales	Ciudad Victoria, Tamps.
Tractomotriz del Norte	Sales	Matamoros, Tamps.
Automóviles	Sales	Monterrey, N.L.
Tubulares Alfa	Sales	Garza García, N.L.
Muebles Infantiles	Sales	Torreón, Coah.
	Other	
Grupo Imsa y Subsidiarias	Industrial groups	Monterrey, N.L.
Automotriz del Norte	Industrial groups	Matamoros, Tamps.
Formet	Industrial groups	San Nicolás de los Garza, N.L.
Fincas Industriales de Monterrey	Services	Monterrey, N.L.
Edisa		Monterrey, N.L.
Multypanel	Prefab. panels	San Nicolás de los Garza, N.L.
Camiones del Noreste		Matamoros, Tamps.
Sujetadores Imsa		San Nicolás de los Garza, N.L.
Camiones y Tracto Camiones		Monterrey, N.L.

Firm	Activity	Location
VISA INDUSTRIAL GROUP		
Aguas de Tehuacán	Beverages	
Aguas y Refrescos de Tehuacán	Beverages	
Cervecería Cuáuhtemoc	Beverages	Monterrey, N.L.
Cervecería Sonora	Beverages	Hermosillo, Son.
Cía. Cervecera de Ciudad Juárez	Beverages	Ciudad Juárez, Chih.
Cía. Cervecera de Chihuahua	Beverages	Chihuahua, Chih.
Delaware Punch	Beverages	México, D.F.
Dist. de Bebidas Valle de México	Beverages	México, D.F.
Embotelladora de Tlanepantla	Beverages	Tlanepantla, Edo. Méx.
Embotelladora del Istmo	Beverages	Tuxtepec, Oax.
Embotelladora sin Rival	Beverages	
Industria Embotelladora de México	Beverages	México, D.F.
Extracción y Embotelladora de Agua Mineral	Beverages	
Manantiales Peñafiel	Beverages	México, D.F.
Jugos Naturales	Beverages	
Productos Balseca	Beverages	
Refrescos Oaxaca	Beverages	Oaxaca, Oax.
Super Calidad	Beverages	
Promotora Oceánica de Atún	Food	
Productos Alimenticios del Mar	Food	
Maya Internacional	Food	
Malta	Food	Monterrey, N.L.
Industrias Mafer del Sur	Food	
Industrias Mafer	Food	Monterrey, N.L.
Alimentos Texo	Food	
Alipe	Food	
Avícola Garrison	Food	
Clemente Jacques y Cía.	Food	Monterrey, N.L.
Desarrollo Avícola Ganadero	Food	
Operadora de Productos Pecuarios	Food	
Paisa	Food	
Quesos La Caperucita	Food	Monterrey, N.L.
Fábricas Monterrey	Metal products	Monterrey, N.L.
Plásticos Técnicos Mexicanos	Plastic products	Monterrey, N.L.
Quimiproductos	Chemicals	
Carplastic	Autoparts	
Grafo Regia	Printing	Monterrey, N.L.
Technohar	Construction	
Agencia Carta Blanca de Tampico	Sales	Tampico, Tamps.
Alimentos y Bebidas de Chiapas	Sales	Chiapas
Bebidas y Alimentos de Oviedo	Sales	
Bier Drive Mexicana	Sales	
Bock	Sales	
Burger Boy	Sales	Monterrey, N.L.
Cadena Comercial	Sales	Monterrey, N.L.
Carta Blanca de Matamoros	Sales	Matamoros, Tamps.

Firm	Activity	Location
Carta Blanca de Nuevo Laredo	Sales	Nuevo Laredo, Tamps.
Carta Blanca de Occidente	Sales	Guadalajara, Jal.
Carta Blanca de Reynosa	Sales	Reynosa, Tamps.
Carta Blanca del Golfo	Sales	Veracruz
Cervecería Cruz Blanca	Sales	Edo. Méx.
Cía. Comercial Distribuidora	Sales	
Dicodelag	Sales	
Distribuidora Comercial Dico	Sales	
Distribuidora de Alimentos y Bebidas Morelos	Sales	Morelos
Distribuidora de Productos Tehuacán	Sales	
Distribuidora del Norte de Coahuila	Sales	Coahuila
Distribuidora de Transistmo	Sales	
Distribución y Reparto	Sales	
Distribuidora Anahuac	Sales	
Distribuidora Cadereyta	Sales	Cadereyta, N.L.
Distribuidora Peñafiel	Sales	
Distribuidora Periférica	Sales	
Distribuidora Sureña	Sales	
First Latin American	Sales	
Fomento Comercial	Sales	
Impulsora de Mercados	Sales	
Mercantil Gastronómica	Sales	
Nueva Icacos	Services	
Operadora Continental de Hoteles	Services	
Grupo Visa	Services	Monterrey, N.L.
Inmobiliaria y Constructora Vadi	Services	
Inmobiliaria y Servicios	Services	
Inmuebles del Golfo	Services	
Inmuebles Industriales del Istmo	Services	
Inmobiliaria Industrial de Tehuacán	Services	
Fomento Económico Mexicano	Services	
Enricar	Services	
Dirección y Servicios	Services	
Disa Inmuebles	Services	
Maquinaria y Vehículos Mavesa	Services	
Propimex	Services	
Servicios Aéreos Regiomontanos	Services	Monterrey, N.L.
Servicios de Administración de Mercados	Services	
Servicios Industriales y Comerciales	Services	
Turismo Visa	Services	
Visa Bioindustrias	Services	
Visa de Monterrey	Services	Monterrey, N.L.
Visa Servicios	Services	
Cía. Operadora La Joya de Acapulco	Hotels & restaurants	Acapulco, Gro.

Firm	Activity	Location
Hoteles Exelaris	Hotels & restaurants	Monterrey, N.L.
Hoteles La Mansión	Hotels & restaurants	
Inmobiliaria Cancún Caribe	Hotels & restaurants	Cancún, Q.R.
Kopay Cadena Hotelera	Hotels & restaurants	
Villas de Galindo	Hotels & restaurants	
Promotora San Gil	Hotels & restaurants	
VITRO INDUSTRIAL GROUP		
Ampolletas	Borosylicate Containers	Querétaro, Qro.
Vidriera Monterrey		Monterrey, N.L.
Shatterproof de México	Automotive glass	México, D.F.
Vidriera Toluca	Glass containers	Toluca, Edo. Méx.
Vidriera Guadalajara	Glass containers	Guadalajara, Jal.
Vidriera Los Reyes	Glass containers	Tlanepantla, Edo. Méx.
Vidriera México	Glass containers	México, D.F.
Vidriera Querétaro	Glass containers	Querétaro, Qro.
Vidrio Neutro	Borosilicate containers	Azcapotzalco, Edo. Méx.
Vidrio Plano de México	Template glass	Izahuatepec, Edo. Méx.
Vitro Fibras	Glass fibers	México, D.F.
Vitro Flex	Automotive glass	Villa de García, N.L.
Vitro Flotado	Template glass	Villa de García, N.L.
Vitro Plan	Glass	Monterrey, N.L.
Vitromatic		Apodaca, N.L.
Vitrocrisa Crimesa	Industrial glass	Monterrey, N.L.
Vitrocrisa Cristalería	Industrial glass	Monterrey, N.L.
Vitrocrisa Kristal	Lead crystal	Monterrey, N.L.
Vitrocrisa Toluca	Glass	Toluca, Edo. Méx.
Vitroplast Monterrey	Plastic containers	Monterrey, N.L.
Cía. General de Plásticos	Plastics	México, D.F.
Productos Kimax	Plastics	
Plásticos Bosco	Plastics	Iztapalapa, Edo. Méx.
Plásticos y Representaciones	Plastics	México, D.F.
Regiomold	Plastics	México, D.F.
Regioplast Guadalajara	Plastics	Guadalajara, Jal.
Peerles Tisa	Oil equipment	Monterrey, N.L.
Quantrón	Nonelectrical machinery	Monterrey, N.L.
Fabricación de Máquinas	Machines & technology	Monterrey, N.L.
Minerales para la Industria	Nonelectrical materials	
Arcillas Tratados	Hydrogel & zeolite	Tlanepantla, Edo. Méx.
Borosilicatos	Nonmetal minerals	Azcapotzalco, Edo. Méx.
Materias Primas Minerales de San José	Nonmetal minerals	Monterrey, N.L.
Materias Primas Minerales de Lampazos	Nonmetal minerals	Lampazos, N.L.
Materias Primas Minerales Magdalena	Nonmetal minerals	
Materias Primas Minerales de Ahuazotepec	Nonmetal minerals	
Silicatos y Derivados	Silicates & Metalsilicates	Tlanepantla, Edo. Méx.

Firm	Activity	Location
Química M	Chemicals	
Industrias Alcali	Chemicals Services	Villa de García, N.L.
Vitro Corporativo	Industrial groups	Monterrey, N.L.
Acción Social Regiomontana	Services	Monterrey, N.L.
Clínica Vidriera	Services	Monterrey, N.L.
Corporación Social	Services	
Fomento Inmobiliario de la Costa Vivir	Services	
Fomento de Comercio Exterior	Services	
Fomexport USA	Services	
Supermatic	Services	Apodaca, N.L.
Valuatec	Services	
Vektron	Services Sales	
Industrias Cornejo	Sales	
Proveedora del Hogar	Sales	

Vitro Firms and Partnerships Abroad

Anchor Glass Container
Latchford Glass
ACI America
World Tableware International*
Corning Incorporates**

* Vitro acquired 49 percent of WTI's Amsilco Division; WTI acquired 49 percent of the Vitrocrisa Division.

**Vitro acquired 49 percent of Corning's Table and Kitchen Ware; Corning acquired 49 percent of Vitro-Corning.

Sources: "Los grupos más importantes de México," *Expansión* 448:18 (September 3, 1986); CAINTRA, *Directorio Industrial de Nuevo León* for 1988, 1990, 1991.

Appendix 2

Plants Visited

CEMEX GROUP

Concretos Monterrey: produces and distributes premixed concrete in the domestic market. The plant has 180 unionized workers.

CYDSA GROUP

Celorey: produces cellophane film and rayon cord. The plant has about 300 workers.

Quimobásicos: manufactures chemical products—primarily propellant gases and sodium bisulfate (used in photo developing, dyes, etc.). Most of its raw materials come from Alcali, a Vitro group affiliate, and Químicas, another Cydsa group firm. The latter is directly connected to Quimobásicos via pipelines. Part of its production is for Crysel, a firm which belongs to the same group, located in Guadalajara, and for Pigmentos y Oxidos (PYOSA). About 25 percent of its production is exported to the United States. The plant has approximately 125 workers and 80 supervisory personnel.

IMSA GROUP

Acumuladores Mexicanos (Acumex): produces automobile batteries. It is 100 percent Mexican capital. Most of its production is for the domestic market, though it does export to the United States and Cuba. There are 630 workers in the plant and 343 supervisory personnel; the plant also employs 882 people in sales.

Cuprum: produces aluminum sections. It is 100 percent Mexican capital and its production is for the domestic market. The plant has 450 workers and 80 supervisory personnel.

Industrias Monterrey (Imsa): produces galvanized sheet metal (Zintro-Pintro). It is 100 percent Mexican capital. Seventy percent of its production goes to the Mexican market, 20 percent to the U.S. market, and 10 percent to Europe and Central and South America. The plant visited has 850 workers and about 500 supervisory personnel.

Vidriera Monterrey: produces glass containers. The plant has 1,900 workers.

OTHER FIRMS

Burroughs Welcome de México: An affiliate of the Welcome Foundation, a pharmaceutical company with 100 percent British capital. However, 98 percent of its production is for the Mexican market, with 2 percent exported to Central America. One of its medium-range objectives is to export from Mexico to Latin America, replacing the activities of a plant in Great Britain in this function. There are 45 workers and 84 supervisory personnel at its plant.

Conek: a subsidiary of Caterpillar in Mexico. It is 100 percent U.S. capital. Manufactures heavy equipment. The plant visited produces primarily forklifts and machinery parts for highway construction and mining equipment. Its production goes to the parent firm in the United States. The plant has 750 workers and close to 550 supervisory personnel.

Appendix 3

Management Boards, 1990

ALFA

Bernando Garza Sada, *President*
Rafael Páez Garza, *General Director*
Rubén Aguilar M.
Antonio Madero Bracho
Alejandro Cumming S.
Rafael Páez Garza
Ernesto Fernández M.
Jacques Regozinski
Armando Garza S.
Enrique Rojas G.
Dionisio Garza Sada
Adrián Sada Treviño
Claudio S. González
Agustín Santamarina
Julio Gutiérrez
Agustín F. Legorreta

CEMEX

Marcelo H. Zambrano, *President*
Lorenzo H. Zambrano T., *General Director*
Lorenzo H. Zambrano T.
Roberto Zambrano W.
Roberto Zambrano L.
Lorenzo Milmo Z.
Armando García S.
Rodolfo García Muriel
Rodolfo F. Barrera V.
Juan F. Muñoz

CYDSA

Andrés Marcelo Sada, *President*
Fernando Sada Malacara, *General Director*
Eugenio Clariond Reyes
Antonio Madero Bracho
Adán Elizondo
Juan F. Muñoz
Alejandro Garza Lagüera
Adrián Sada Treviño
Bernardo Garza Sada
Adrián Sada González
Raúl González Quiroz
Tomás González Sada
Adrián Sada Zambrano
Javier López del Bosque
Gerardo Sada Zambrano

IMSA

Eugenio Clariond Garza, *President*
Eugenio Clariond Reyes, *General Director*
Fernando Canales Clariond
Santiago Clariond Reyes
Benjamín Clariond Reyes
Marcelo Canales Clariond

VISA

Eugenio Garza Lagüera, *President*
Othón Ruiz Montemayor, *General Director*
Ricardo Guajardo Touche
Jesús Flores Treviño
Eduardo Bermúdez Santos
Héctor Lazo Hinojosa

VITRO

Adrián Sada Treviño, *President*
Ernesto Martens, *General Director*
Adrián Sada González
Adolfo Larralde
Eduardo G. Brittingham
Dionisio Garza Sada
Mario Garza G.
Tomás González Sada
Pablo González Sada
Juan F. Muñoz
Federico Garza Sada

Appendix 4

CPNL Proposal for Reform of Constitutional Article 123

1. We propose eliminating the term "day worker" from Article 123 because it is obsolete.

2. Section I: We recommend establishing an obligatory 48-hour workweek distributed according to the wishes of the parties involved.

3. Section II: We recommend removing the maximum limit on the length of a night shift.

4. Section III: We recommend setting twelve years of age as the minimum age for employment, and that for workers under the age of fourteen the workweek be limited to 36 hours and the workday to 6 hours.

5. Section V: We recommend reducing prenatal maternity leave to three weeks, and also that the inclusion of a breast-feeding period be eliminated from this section, since fewer and fewer mothers are nursing their infants.

6. Section VI: The daily minimum wage must give way to an hourly wage. We recommend setting a single minimum wage base for all of Mexico and eliminating the professional minimum wage.

7. Section IX: We recommend that the basis on which profits are distributed be a worker's wage, not days of attendance. We recommend establishing a ceiling on the amount of distributable profit.

8. Section XI: We propose that hours worked in excess of 48 hours be considered overtime hours, to be paid at twice the regular wage.

9. Section XII: Because of current demands on labor, we recommend that training be a normal part of a worker's schedule.

10. Section XVI: We recommend replacing "etcetera" with "or analogous ones."

11. Section XVIII: We recommend extending to workers at all private firms the stipulation now required of public-service workers that they give a 10-day advance notification to the Conciliation and Arbitration Board of the date fixed for a work stoppage or strike.

12. Section XXI: It must be made clear that when it is the workers who refuse to submit to the board's arbitration or accept arbitration decisions, the work contract shall end, with no responsibility on the employer's part. It is understood that this section shall not apply if there is unemployment insurance. An employer may lay off workers without incurring any responsibility when workers fail to meet job specifications as agreed on by worker and employer.

13. Section XXII: We propose that this section also specify that the employer may, without incurring any responsibility, rescind the contract of any worker who participates in a strike that has been declared illegal.

14. Section XXVI: We propose that this section be eliminated.

15. Section XXVII, Clause C: We propose replacing "day wage" with "wage."

16. We propose doing away with Apartado B, so that there is a single constitutional rule covering all workers whether or not they are government employees.

Acronyms List

BANOBRAS	Banco Nacional de Obras Públicas/National Public Works Bank
CAINTRA	Cámara de la Industria de Transformación/Chamber of Manufacturers
CANACINTRA	Cámara Nacional de la Industria de Transformación/National Chamber of Manufacturers
CCE	Comité Coordinador Empresarial/Business Coordinating Council
COPARMEX	Confederación Patronal de la República Mexicana/Business Federation of Mexico
COR	Confederación de Obreros Revolucionarios/Revolutionary Labor Federation
CPNL	Centro Patronal de Nuevo León/Nuevo León Employers' Center
CTM	Confederación de Trabajadores de México/Confederation of Mexican Workers
FENSI	Federación Nacional de Sindicatos Independientes/National Federation of Independent Trade Unions
FICORCA	Fideicomiso para la Cobertura de Riesgo Cambiario/Exchange Rate Risk Trust Fund
FTSA	Federación de Trabajadores de Sindicatos Autónomos/Federation of Workers' in Autonomous Trade Unions
IMF	International Monetary Fund
IMSS	Instituto Mexicano del Seguro Social/Mexican Social Security Institute

INFONAVIT	Instituto del Fondo Nacional de la Vivienda para los Trabajadores/Fund for National Workers' Housing
ISSSTE	Instituto de Seguridad y Servicios Sociales de los Trabajadores del Estado/Social Security Institute for State Workers
PAC	Programa de Aliento y Crecimiento/Stimulus and Growth Program
PAN	Partido de Acción Nacional/National Action Party
PECE	Pacto para la Estabilidad y Crecimiento Económico/Pact for Stability and Economic Growth
PIRE	Programa Inmediato de Recuperación Económica/Economic Recovery Program
PRONAFICE	Programa Nacional de Fomento al Comercio Exterior/National Program to Promote Foreign Trade
PSE	Pacto de Solidaridad Económica/Economic Solidarity Pact

References

Armstrong, J.A. 1991. Televised conference, Xerox Corporation Research and Development Department.

BANAMEX (Banco Nacional de México). 1987. *México Social 1987.* Mexico: Departamento de Asuntos Sociales, Banco Nacional de México.

Bennett, Vivienne. 1987. "Urban Water Services and Social Conflicts: The Water Crisis in Monterrey, Mexico, 1973–1985." Ph.D. dissertation, University of Texas at Austin.

Boyer, Robert. 1987. "The Eighties: The Search for Alternatives to Fordism." Paper presented at the Sixth Annual Conference of Europeanists, November.

———. 1988. "Entrevista," *Investigación Económica* (Universidad Nacional Autónoma de México) 183 (January–March).

———. 1990. "La informatización de la producción y la polivalencia." In *La ocupación del futuro*, edited by Esthela Gutiérrez. Mexico: Fundación Friedrich Ebert/Nueva Sociedad.

Carrillo, Jorge. 1985. *Conflictos laborales en la industria maquiladora.* Tijuana: Centro de Estudios Fronterizos del Norte de México.

———. 1988. "Dos décadas del sindicalismo en la industria maquiladora de exportación: examen de Tijuana, Ciudad Juárez y Matamoros." Master's thesis, Universidad Nacional Autónoma de México.

Carrillo, Jorge, ed. 1990. *La nueva era de la industria automotriz en México.* Tijuana: El Colegio de la Frontera Norte.

Cerutti, Mario. 1983. *Burguesía y capitalismo en Monterrey, 1850–1910.* Mexico: Claves Latinoamericanas.

CIDE (Centro de Investigaciones para el Desarrollo). 1989. *Tecnología e industria en el futuro de México.* Mexico: Diana.

CIEN (Centro de Información y Estudios Nacionales). 1983. Archival data.

Clariond Reyes, Eugenio. 1990. "Cumbre 1990. Los retos de la apertura." Special supplement to *El Norte*, November 26.

CNSM (Comisión Nacional de Salarios Mínimos). 1989. *Compendio de indicadores de empleo y salarios*, December. Mexico: CNSM.

Comercio Exterior. 1985. "Recuento Nacional," 35:8 (August): 769–73.

De la Garza, Enrique. 1988. "Desindustrialización y reconversión en México," *El Cotidiano*, January–February.

————. 1992. "El Tratado de Libre Comercio de América del Norte y las relaciones laborales en México." In *Ajuste estructural, mercados laborales y el TLC*. Mexico: El Colegio de México/Fundación Friedrich Ebert/El Colegio de la Frontera Norte.

Destler, I.M. 1992. *American Trade Politics*. 2d ed. Washington, D.C.: Institute for International Economics; New York: Twentieth Century Fund.

Dosi, Giovanni. 1982. "Technological Paradigms and Technological Trajectories," *Research Policy* 11.

Expansión. 1983. "El dilema de los regiomontanos. Lo que la crisis se llevó," 15:381 (December 21): 48–55.

————. 1986. "¿Qué tanto importan las exportaciones?" 18:432 (January 15): 54–60.

————. 1987. "¿Quién pagará la deuda privada?" 19:464 (April 29): 19–21.

————. 1989. "Los grupos más importantes de México," 21:523 (August 30): 35–44.

————. 1992a. "Indicador empresarial. Optimismo con Nubarrones," 24:595 (July 22): 40.

————. 1992b. "Cemex: el imperio se fortalece," 24:593 (June 24): 68.

Gambrill, Mónica. 1990. "Sindicalismo en las maquiladoras de Tijuana. Regresión en las prestaciones sociales." In *Reestructuración industrial: las maquiladoras en la frontera México-Estados Unidos*. Mexico: Consejo Nacional para la Cultura y las Artes/El Colegio de la Frontera Norte.

Garrido, Celso, et al. 1987. "Crisis y poder en México: un ensayo de interpretación," *Estudios Sociológicos* 5:15.

Garrido, Celso, and Nancy Quintana. 1988. "Crisis del patrón de acumulación y modernización conservadora del capitalismo en México."In *Empresarios y Estado en América Latina*. Mexico: Centro de Investigación y Docencia Económicas/Fundación Friedrich Ebert/Universidad Autónoma Metropolitana.

Garza, Alma Rosa, and Efraín Pérez. 1984. "El movimiento de posesionarios en Monterrey, 1970–1983. Monterrey, N.L. Mimeo.

Gertler, Mark. 1988. "The Limits to Flexibility: Comments on the Post-Fordist Vision of Production and Its Geography," *Transactions of the Institute of British Geographers* 13.

Glyn, A.; A. Hughes; A. Lipietz; and A. Singh. 1988. "The Rise and Fall of the Golden Age." In *The Golden Age of Capitalism*, edited by Stepehn Marglin and Juliet Schor. Oxford: Oxford University Press.

Hualde, A., and J. Micheli. 1988. "Un overol teórico para la reconversión,"*El Cotidiano* 21 (January–February).

Ibarra, J. 1984. "El movimiento universitario por la autonomía y la democracia en la UANL." Monterrey, N.L. OIDMO. Mimeo.

INEGI (Instituto Nacional de Estadística, Geografía e Informática). 1992. Archival information.

Kalifa, Salvador.' 1990. "Cumbre 90. Los retos de la apertura." Special supplement to *El Norte*, November 26.

Leborgne, Dominique, and Alain Lipietz. 1988. "New Technologies, New Modes of Regulation: Some Spatial Implications," *Environment and Planning D: Society and Space*.

Locke, R. 1990. "In Search of Flexibility: Industrial Restructuring and Industrial Relations in the Italian Automobile Industry." Cambridge: Massachusetts Institute of Technology. Mimeo.

Mahon, Rianne. 1987. "From Fordism to?: New Technology, Labour Markets and Unions," *Economic and Industrial Democracy* 6.

Marglin, Stephen A. 1974. "What Do Bosses Do? The Origins and Functions of Hierarchy in Capitalist Production," *Review of Radical and Political Economics*, Summer.

Micheli, Jordi. 1991. "Nueva manufactura, globalización y producción de automóviles en México." Typescript.

Middlebrook, Kevin J. 1991. "The Politics of Industrial Restructuring. Transnational Firms' Search for Flexible Production in the Mexican Automobile Industry," *Comparative Politics* 23:3 (April).

Nuncio, Abraham. 1982. *El Grupo Monterrey*. Mexico: Nueva Imagen.

———. 1984. "Las organizaciones empresariales en Monterrey: expresión de una burguesía militante." Monterrey, N.L.: OIDMO. Mimeo.

Páez, Rafael. 1990. "Cumbre 90. Los retos de la apertura." Special supplement to *El Norte*, November 26.

Piore, Michael. 1990. "Dos concepciones sobre la flexibilidad del trabajo." In *La ocupación del futuro*, edited by Esthela Gutiérrez. Mexico: Fundación Friedrich Ebert/Nueva Sociedad.

Piore, Michael, and Charles Sabel. 1985. *The Second Industrial Divide: Possibilities for Prosperity*. New York: Basic Books.

Pozas, María A. 1990. "Estrategias empresariales ante la apertura externa." In *Subcontratación y empresas transnacionales*, edited by

Bernardo González Aréchiga and J.C. Ramírez. Mexico: El Colegio de la Frontera Norte/Fundación Friedrich Ebert.

————. 1992a. "Modernización de las relaciones laborales en las empresas regiomontanas." In *Ajuste estructural, mercados de trabajo y el TLC*. Mexico: El Colegio de México/Fundación Friedrich Ebert/El Colegio de la Frontera Norte.

————. 1992b. *Restructuración industrial en Monterrey*. Documentos de Trabajo, no. 40. Mexico: Fundación Friedrich Ebert.

————. 1993. "Problemas de la innovación y la transferencia tecnológica en las empresas regiomontanas." In *Tecnología y reconversión productiva. El reto de fin de siglo*. Mexico: Universidad Autónoma Metropolitana-Xochimilco.

Progreso. 1991. "Principales exportadores en América Latina," August 18.

Quintero, Cirila. 1990. *La sindicalización en las maquiladoras tijuanenses*. Mexico: Consejo Nacional para la Cultura y las Artes.

————. 1991. "Reestructuración sindical en las maquiladoras. El caso de Agapito González Cavasos." Mimeo.

Rojas, Javier. 1983. "Los sindicatos blancos de Monterrey: un modelo patronal de organización sindical." Thesis, Universidad Autónoma de Nuevo León.

Roldán, Martha. 1992. "Un debate pendiente: innovaciones tecnológicas blandas, reconversión industrial y desregulación en el contexto latinoamericano de los 90. Hacia una perspectiva sensible al género." Paper presented to the XVII International Congress of the Latin American Studies Association, September, Los Angeles, California.

Ruiz-Montemayor, Othón. 1990. "Cumbre 90. Los retos de la apertura." Special supplement to *El Norte*, November 26.

Saragoza, Alexander M. 1988. *The Monterrey Elite and the Mexican State, 1880–1940*. Austin: University of Texas Press.

Schoenberger, Erica. 1989a. "Some Dilemmas of Automation: Strategic and Operational Aspects of Technological Change in Production," *Economic Geography* 65:3 (July).

————. 1989b. "Thinking about Flexibility: A Response to Gertler," *Transactions of the Institute of British Geographers* 14.

SECOFI (Secretaría de Comercio y Fomento Industrial). 1992. Archival data.

Shaiken, Harley. 1990. *Mexico in the Global Economy: High Technology and Work Organization in Export Industries*. Monograph Series, no. 33. La Jolla: Center for U.S.-Mexican Studies, University of California, San Diego.

Simon, C. 1990. "New Utopias for Old: Fordist Dreams and Post-Fordist Fantasies," *Capital and Class* 42.

About the Author

María de los Angeles Pozas is a researcher at El Colegio de la Frontera Norte in Monterrey, Mexico, and a member of the faculty at the Universidad Autónoma de Nuevo León. Her research over the last several years has focused on the steps that Mexican industry is taking in response to the opening of the Mexican economy and that country's increasing integration with the North American economy. During 1991–92 Pozas was a Visiting Fellow at the Center for U.S.-Mexican Studies, UCSD, during which period she wrote up her research on the restructuring of six major industrial groups in Monterrey; the resulting volume was awarded the 1992 Prize for Research in the Social Sciences of the Universidad Autónoma de Nuevo León. With grant support from Mexico's National Science and Technology Council, she is currently conducting a comparative study on the alterations in work organization caused by the introduction of technological innovation in industrial firms in several regions of Mexico. Pozas is also a member of a research team funded by Canada's International Development Research Centre (IDRC) to conduct a comparative study of the impacts of introducing labor flexibility in the industrial workplace in several Latin American countries.